I0821850

Handling
Depression

by Marie-Therese Miller, PhD

Content Consultant
Dr. Carla Marie Manly
Clinical Psychologist and
Wellness Expert

Handling
Health Challenges

Essential Library
An Imprint of Abdo Publishing
abdobooks.com

abdobooks.com

Published by Abdo Publishing, a division of ABDO, PO Box 398166, Minneapolis, Minnesota 55439.

Printed in the United States of America, North Mankato, Minnesota.
052021
092021

Cover Photo: Dean Drobot/Shutterstock Images
Interior Photos: iStockphoto, 4, 6, 10–11, 20, 38, 47, 50, 55, 89; Monkey Business Images/Shutterstock Images, 9; Shutterstock Images, 16, 30, 43; Kosim Shukurov/Shutterstock Images, 26; Marc Bruxelle/iStockphoto, 33; James King-Holmes/Science Source, 59; Dmytro Zinkevych/Shutterstock Images, 64; Alfred Pasieka/Science Source, 66; Dr P. Marazzi/Science Source, 69, 98; Leonid Iastremskyi/Pixel-shot/Alamy, 71; Will & Deni McIntyre/Science Source, 76–77; Brian Niles/iStockphoto, 80; Motortion Films/Shutterstock Images, 84; Antonio Perez/Chicago Tribune/Tribune News Service/Getty Images, 90; Martin Bond/Science Source, 93

Editor: Arnold Ringstad
Series Designer: Megan Ellis

Library of Congress Control Number: 2020948036

Publisher's Cataloging-in-Publication Data

Names: Miller, Marie-Therese, author.
Title: Handling depression / by Marie-Therese Miller, PhD
Description: Minneapolis, Minnesota : Abdo Publishing, 2022 | Series: Handling health challenges | Includes online resources and index.
Identifiers: ISBN 9781532194962 (lib. bdg.) | ISBN 9781098215279 (ebook)
Subjects: LCSH: Depression, Mental--Juvenile literature. | Depressed persons--Juvenile literature. | Depression, Mental--Social aspects--Juvenile literature. | Depression, Mental--Diagnosis--Juvenile literature. | Depression, Mental--Treatment--Juvenile literature. | Health--Juvenile literature.
Classification: DDC 362.25--dc23

Contents

Trigger warning: This book presents scenarios and discussions involving suicide and self-harm.

Chapter One

What Is Depression?

Lily spread her music on the stand and tuned her cello. Her hands were shaking a bit with nerves as she began to perform her Bach piece. It was the end of her junior year in high school, and she was auditioning for the most advanced orchestra in her school. When she played the final note, her orchestra teacher congratulated her. Lily had been accepted! Performing at this level would require many hours of practicing, but she was willing to put in the hard work.

Lily had been playing the cello since fourth grade. Everything about the cello made her happy: taking lessons, playing in ensembles, and practicing all types of music, from classical to pop. She didn't even mind lugging the instrument on her back. It was as natural to her as a shell on a tortoise.

One effect of depression can be a loss of interest in one's favorite activities, such as playing music.

Someone dealing with depression may not want to leave his or her bed and start the day.

During the summer before Lily's senior year, she had a lot of music to practice. Her dream was to attend college for cello performance, so she had to prepare for many college auditions. She practiced each day, taking breaks to go swimming or see movies with friends. Lily practically lived for scary movies.

But as July wore on, Lily found practicing the cello was more of a chore than a joy. "The cello isn't fun anymore," she told her parents. She started to sleep late into the afternoon every day. Her older sisters tried to lure her away from her bed with promises of shopping or chocolate milkshakes, her favorite treats, but Lily only wanted to stay in her room alone. She didn't even go out to restaurants or the bowling alley with her friends anymore. "I'm just too exhausted," she told them.

The Diagnosis

Her parents were worried and took her to the doctor. Lily had X-rays and blood work done. No medical problems were found. Then, the doctor recommended that a psychiatrist might be able to help.

Lily was very reluctant to see the psychiatrist. "I don't think a psychiatrist will help me," she said. "No one can help me." But one day, she confided in her mom that she wished she would fall asleep and not wake up again. Her mother made an appointment with the psychiatrist right away.

The psychiatrist diagnosed Lily with major depressive disorder. She prescribed the antidepressant medication paroxetine. However, a side effect of the medication left Lily feeling sleepier. The psychiatrist explained that switching medications is common, since they affect people differently. She weaned Lily off paroxetine and prescribed fluoxetine instead. The doctor told Lily that the medication might take a few weeks to work. She had to be patient.

In six weeks, she was sleeping less and had more energy. Her stomach felt better, and her appetite returned. Lily was also seeing a psychologist for cognitive behavioral therapy. The psychologist taught her many coping skills, such as mindfulness. Lily was exercising daily, going on regular bike rides. She was eating healthful foods—more apples, fewer doughnuts. She was also keeping to a regular sleep schedule, just as her psychologist recommended.

A few more weeks passed, and Lily's mood began to brighten. She was able to concentrate on schoolwork. Once again, she felt joy when she played the cello, and she performed her college auditions. When she got word that she was accepted to her top college choice, her friends took her out to celebrate with chocolate milkshakes and a scary movie.

How Family and Friends Can Help

Psychologist Michelle Quilter advises family members and friends to be available to and listen to the person with depression. Quilter says, "Reach out to the person and let her talk if she wants. However, be careful not to obsessively focus on the depression."[1] The nonjudgmental support of family and friends is vital to someone facing the challenges of depression.

Symptoms of Depression

Major depression, often referred to by medical

With treatment, people with depression can overcome their symptoms and enjoy life again.

professionals as clinical depression, is one of the most common mental disorders in the United States. It is sometimes called depression for short. The disorder affects a person's emotional state. Many people have sad days now and then, but the mental health diagnosis of depression means the individual experiences persistent sadness or continuous low mood. People with depression lose interest in activities they once enjoyed.

Depression interferes with a person's everyday life. It can affect performance at work or at school. It might cause problems in interpersonal relationships with family, friends, and colleagues. Depression can make it difficult to do the most ordinary things, such

Talking to a mental health professional is often the first step in getting help for depression.

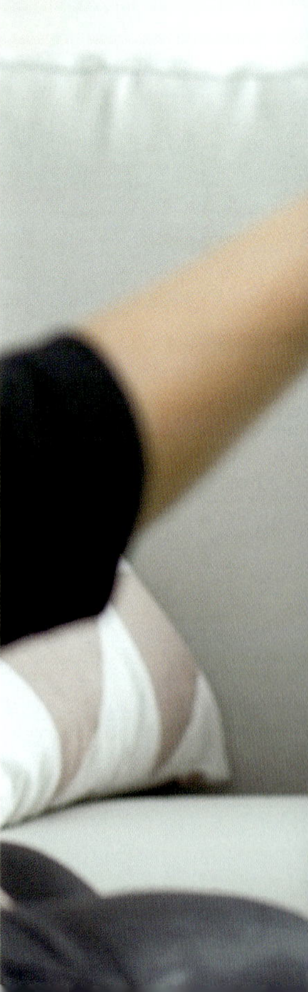

as taking a shower or fixing a meal. Depression might be life-threatening because individuals with depression can have suicidal thoughts, known as suicidal ideation. Some individuals with depression try to end their own lives.

Finding Help

A person experiencing depressive symptoms can visit a mental health professional for help. Mental health professionals are specially trained to diagnose and treat mental health disorders. Taking the first step toward obtaining this help can be difficult. Sometimes a person with depression is reluctant to seek professional help because the very symptoms of the disorder get in the way. He might lack the energy to make it to the appointment. He might not be optimistic about the outcome of treatment. In his book *Depression: A*

Guide for The Newly Diagnosed, psychologist Lee H. Coleman offers this advice: "You may feel skeptical or even pessimistic that anything can help you. . . . Even if you're feeling pessimistic, consider that it may be the depression itself that is making you pessimistic, and so it may take treating the disorder first in order to change your thinking."[2]

There are many ways to find a qualified mental health professional. People can ask their health-care providers to suggest mental health professionals that the providers would choose for their own mental health or for the mental health of their family members. Qualified mental health professionals can also be located through professional organizations, such as the American Psychiatric Association or the American Psychological Association. Family members and trusted friends may recommend mental health professionals too.

There are a variety of mental health professionals, and it is helpful to understand the differences between them. Psychiatrists are doctors who have attended medical school. In addition, they have undergone an additional four years of training in their specialty. Psychiatrists diagnose and treat mental illness. They can prescribe and manage medication, making certain that the proper medication in effective doses is being administered. Some psychiatrists offer psychotherapy, also known as talk therapy. If deciding whether to choose a family physician or psychiatrist for treatment of depression, Coleman advises, "Depression is just a small part of what family physicians see day to day, whereas psychiatrists see many more people who are depressed and can usually bring more experience to your care."[3]

A licensed psychologist holds a doctorate in psychology, such as a PhD or PsyD. They are specialists in testing, diagnosis, and psychotherapy. Psychologists in five states—New Mexico, Louisiana, Illinois, Iowa, and Idaho—can receive additional training in order to prescribe medication to treat mental illness. There are also psychologists working for the US Department of Defense, the US Public Health Service, and the Indian Health Service that can prescribe

More Mental Health Specialists

Psychiatric mental health advance practice registered nurses (PMH-APRN) have a master's or doctoral degree and can diagnose mental illness, prescribe medicine, and offer therapy. Marriage and family therapists (MFT) and licensed clinical social workers (LCSW) hold at least a master's degree in their specialty and can diagnose mental illness and offer psychotherapy.

medication. However, in most states, psychologists are not permitted to write prescriptions for medication.

Protecting Privacy

People should feel safe when sharing their experiences with their mental health providers. Mental health professionals are required to keep what a client tells them private. This is known as confidentiality. In the United States, the Health Insurance Portability and Accountability Act of 1996 (HIPAA) includes a privacy rule to ensure confidentiality. Individual states have additional laws to protect privacy. However, if the client is a danger to herself or to others, confidentiality may be waived to protect people from harm.

The First Step in Diagnosis

The first step in the diagnosis of depression is to rule out possible medical causes. Many medical conditions have depression as a symptom, and an effort to detect these must occur before a diagnosis of a mental disorder is made. The diagnosis of a medical illness may include a variety of tests and will likely include blood work and urinalysis. A magnetic resonance imaging (MRI) scan may be ordered in some cases.

Depressive symptoms are often noted in patients who have had a stroke or traumatic brain injury. Parkinson's disease and Huntington's disease are also linked to depression. Endocrine disorders such as hypothyroidism, in which not enough thyroid hormone is produced by the thyroid, and Cushing's disease, in which the body has too much of the hormone cortisol, can produce depressive symptoms too. People with anemia, a condition in which a person has too few red blood cells, can also experience depression.

> "Psychologists use psychological testing to help make a reliable, evidence-based diagnosis."[4]
>
> *—Psychologist Michelle Quilter*

If an underlying medical condition is found, it can be treated and the depressive symptoms may resolve. On the other hand, if no underlying medical condition that could cause depressive symptoms is uncovered, the mental health professional may proceed to make a depression diagnosis. There are several types of diagnoses. Whichever type of depression an individual has, it poses a difficult challenge to her everyday life. However, many effective treatment options exist today, and new ones are in development. The outcomes for many of those diagnosed with depression are positive.

Chapter Two

Major and Persistent Depressive Disorders

Mental health professionals use the *Diagnostic and Statistical Manual of Mental Disorders, Fifth Edition (DSM-5)* to guide them in diagnosing depression. This manual is published by the American Psychiatric Association and draws upon the expertise of hundreds of international mental health experts. The *DSM-5* lists several categories of depressive disorders. They include major depressive disorder, persistent depressive disorder, premenstrual dysphoric disorder, substance/medication-induced depressive disorder, depressive disorder due to another medical condition, and disruptive mood dysregulation disorder. Each of

When making a diagnosis, mental health professionals take note of how symptoms match up with the criteria in the *DSM-5*.

> "Unlike physical disabilities, persons with mental illnesses are perceived by the public to be in control of their disabilities and responsible for causing them."[1]
>
> *—Patrick W. Corrigan, professor of psychology, and Amy C. Watson, professor of social work, on the stigma of mental illness*

these depressive disorders includes criteria, such as symptoms and time frame, which must be met to arrive at that particular diagnosis.

Major Depressive Disorder

For major depressive disorder to be diagnosed, the *DSM-5* has a grouping of symptoms that must be evident in the individual for at least two weeks. At least five of those symptoms must be present. In addition, these symptoms have to cause significant disruption in everyday life. The symptoms might interfere with personal relationships, with work, or with school. In order to arrive at the diagnosis of major depressive disorder, the symptoms must be present on most days. Once the diagnosis is made, mental health professionals will determine its severity. The depression can be diagnosed as mild, moderate, or severe.

One of the symptoms of major depressive disorder is having a depressed mood. The person might feel sad much of the time and might cry often. She might be without hope or feel helpless. Sometimes the individual describes feeling empty or feeling nothing at all. The person may experience physical symptoms, such as intestinal disturbances and muscle aches. Some people with depressed mood can act very irritable when faced with minor annoyances.

People with major depressive disorder often do not find pleasure in activities that they once enjoyed. For example, a person might have been an avid snowboarder but the sport doesn't hold any excitement for him anymore. Perhaps the person used

Prevalence of Major Depressive Disorder

Major depressive disorder is a common mental illness in the United States. According to data from the National Health and Nutrition Examination Survey, 8.1 percent of US adults 20 years old and older had major depression in a given two-week period between 2013 and 2016.[2] More women than men had major depression. The prevalence of major depression decreased as income increased. In other words, there are more cases of depression among people with lower income. The *DSM-5* notes that major depressive disorder can occur at any age, but in the United States, most people are diagnosed in their twenties.

A loss of appetite, leading to weight loss, may be one result of depression.

to love his job as an elementary school music teacher, but he can barely smile at his class of second graders.

Those with major depressive disorder can experience a change in eating habits. They might have a loss of appetite and eat less than they usually did. On the other hand, they might eat more. The *DSM-5* notes that a weight change of 5 percent, either gained or lost, within a month can be considered a symptom of major depressive disorder.

Another symptom of major depressive disorder is a change in sleep patterns. Some people sleep too much, known as hypersomnia. Others experience insomnia, which is having trouble sleeping. They could have difficulty falling asleep or might wake from sleep and not be able to fall back to sleep.

The way a person moves or talks can change in major depressive disorder. The individual's actions might be slower. For example, she could walk or talk more slowly. Her speech might be quieter, or she might speak using fewer words. Her voice might be more monotone with fewer vocal variations. Other people with major depressive disorder may start to move more. They might pace around the room or wring their hands, for instance. A person may experience a loss of energy. He might talk about feeling fatigued or tired. The *DSM-5* explains, "An individual might complain that washing and dressing in the morning are exhausting and take twice as long as usual."[3]

Major depressive disorder affects how a person feels about himself. He might feel worthless, as if he has nothing of value to offer to others or to the community. He can experience intense feelings of guilt for simple or inconsequential mistakes. Major depressive disorder can also affect people's thinking. They might have difficulty concentrating or remembering things. Organizing tasks can prove tricky. Some people with this disorder have trouble making decisions, even relatively simple decisions such as choosing an outfit to wear or deciding what to cook for dinner.

> "Depression isn't the result of a character flaw. It's not laziness. It's not simply a case of the blues. And people who are depressed aren't faking it, and they can no more snap out of their depression than individuals with diabetes or arthritis can snap out of their illness."[4]
>
> *—Psychiatrist Keith Kramlinger of the Mayo Clinic, a leading US hospital*

People with major depressive disorder might have suicidal ideation. Some may consider their own death passively. For example, they might wish to go to sleep and not awaken. Other people with this disorder think more seriously about actively killing themselves. Some people plan their suicide. They might consider a method, time, and location. Some individuals with major depressive disorder kill themselves. The disorder, therefore, can be life-threatening. Any suicidal thought patterns and related behaviors should be taken very seriously.

Persistent Depressive Disorder (Dysthymia)

Another depressive disorder diagnosis is persistent depressive disorder, also known as dysthymia.

According to the *DSM-5*, individuals with persistent depressive disorder have a depressed mood for more than two years. Their sad mood must be experienced for the majority of days during that time. For children and teenagers, the required time frame is only one year. The depressed mood for that age group might be expressed as irritability rather than sadness. The mental health professional will determine whether the persistent depressive disorder is mild, moderate, or severe.

The symptoms listed in the *DSM-5* for this disorder are similar to those of major depressive disorder, but fewer of them are required for a diagnosis. To meet this diagnosis, a person must have at least two of the symptoms. A person with persistent depressive disorder might have a change in eating or sleeping habits. She could lack energy or feel fatigued.

An individual with persistent depressive disorder might have low self-esteem. Self-esteem is how a person values himself. Someone with low self-esteem often views himself as not valuable. He might believe that he is not lovable or has no talents to offer, for example. Another symptom of this disorder is a difficulty with concentration or decision-making.

Feeling hopeless is the *DSM*'s last listed symptom of dysthymia.

It is possible for a person to be diagnosed with both persistent depressive disorder and major depressive disorder. The *DSM-5* explains, "Individuals whose symptoms meet major depressive disorder criteria for 2 years should be given a diagnosis of persistent depressive disorder as well as major depressive disorder."[5]

Is It Grief or Depression?

Grief is the feeling of deep sadness in response to a loss. There are many types of loss that lead to grief. People grieve for loved ones who have died. They can also feel grief when going through a relationship breakup, losing a job, being diagnosed with a serious medical issue, or having significant financial problems. It is important for mental health professionals to consider a person's life situation when they are diagnosing depression. They need to differentiate between a normal grief reaction and a diagnosis of depression.

Psychologist Michelle Quilter, director of the dialectical behavior therapy (DBT) program at Lifeskills South Florida, says, "Feeling depressed is part of the grief process."[6] Grieving people may feel sad, have trouble getting out of bed, have difficulty eating, and sometimes consider suicide. One of the differences between grief and major depression is the length of time they last. According to the *DSM-5*, grief lasts from two to six months, whereas depressive disorders often last longer.

In addition, Quilter explains, "Grief has its ups and downs. Depression is a more consistent low mood."[7] A grieving person can find joy in some situations, which is less likely for those with depression. Also, people experiencing grief do not normally feel worthless or guilty, but people with depression often do. With all this said, it is possible for a grieving person to be diagnosed with depression as well.

Stigma

Societal stigma about mental disorders exists. This means there is often a negative view of those diagnosed with mental disorders. For example, some people mistakenly believe that mental disorders cause those diagnosed to be more violent. Others incorrectly consider a mental disorder diagnosis to be a sign of personal weakness. When stigma is present, it can damage relationships or be the cause of discrimination at work, at school, or in social settings. Stigma can even affect the way people with mental disorders feel about themselves. Talking openly about mental disorders is one way to counter this stigma.

Chapter Three

Other Depressive Disorders

The *DSM-5* discusses several additional depressive disorders beyond major depressive disorder and persistent depressive disorder. One of these is premenstrual dysphoric disorder. This type of depression is linked to the hormonal cycle of people who menstruate. The symptoms usually begin about one week before menstruation and completely disappear a few days after menstruation has begun.

Someone must experience at least five symptoms from two different symptom lists to be diagnosed with this disorder. From the first list, she must have at least one mood symptom. The mood symptoms include mood swings, irritability or anger, depressed mood, and anxiety. A person must also have at

Some depressive disorders are linked to factors such as menstruation, substance use, and medical conditions.

least one symptom from the second grouping of symptoms. The second list has much in common with other depressive disorders, and it includes changes in sleep and eating habits, decreased interest in once-enjoyed activities, fatigue, and difficulty concentrating. The person with premenstrual dysphoric disorder might feel overwhelmed. She could also experience physical symptoms, such as tender breasts and abdominal bloating.

Perimenopause and Depression

The time before menstruation stops completely is called perimenopause. During perimenopause, the levels of the hormones estrogen and progesterone are declining. Changes in these hormones are linked to depression. Jennifer Payne, MD, notes the connection between these hormones and depression: "When women go through sudden hormonal changes like those that come with perimenopause, puberty, postpartum, and even their monthly cycle, they're at higher risk for depression."[1]

Those in perimenopause can also have sleep disturbances that may be caused by night sweats. Interrupted sleep is linked to a lowering of mood. In addition, perimenopause occurs at a time when there are frequent life changes. For example, someone in perimenopause might have children moving away from home. Lifestyle changes such as coping with an empty nest can be difficult to manage.

Sometimes, hormonal medication can be helpful to fight perimenopausal depression. However, Payne advises that if the diagnosis is major depressive disorder, antidepressant medication and psychotherapy are probably the best treatment options.

Many people who menstruate experience some of the symptoms of premenstrual dysphoric disorder due to the monthly changes in their hormones. However, to receive this diagnosis the symptoms must cause a significant disruption to a person's life. Doctors Sabrina Hofmeister and Seth Bodden note, "About 80% of women report at least one physical or psychiatric symptom during the luteal phase [the time after ovulation] of their menstrual cycle; however, most do not report significant impairment in their daily life."[2] The prevalence of premenstrual dysphoric disorder is between 1.3 percent and 5.3 percent of women in a 12-month period.[3]

"It is essential to maintain a regular routine and structure to each day, even when you don't feel like it."[4]

—Susan J. Noonan, author of *Managing Your Depression: What You Can Do to Feel Better*

Mental health professionals face the challenge of differentiating between a diagnosis of premenstrual dysphoric disorder and another cyclical disorder linked to the menstrual cycle called premenstrual syndrome. Premenstrual syndrome does not require as many symptoms for its diagnosis. It also does not require a mood symptom to be present.

Substance/Medication-Induced Depressive Disorder

Many illicit drugs and prescription medications are linked to depressive symptoms. For this reason, mental health professionals must consider what substances or illicit drugs a person might have

Alcohol is among the substances that can worsen a person's depression.

taken or what medications he has been prescribed. These substances might be causing his depression. The *DSM-5* offers the category substance/medication-induced depressive disorder for this possibility. The person must experience depressed mood and lack of interest in most activities to be diagnosed with this disorder. He will likely demonstrate additional symptoms similar to those of other depressive disorders. The lifetime prevalence of this diagnosis in the United States is 0.26 percent.[5]

Involuntary Commitment

To help a person who is gravely mentally ill get treatment, mental health providers, health-care providers, and law enforcement may admit that person into the hospital without his or her consent. This is called involuntary commitment. US states allow for involuntary commitment under specific circumstances. The considerations for commitment include whether the person is a clear and present danger to himself or others, and, in some states, whether the person is able to make care and treatment choices on his own.

Often illicit drug use can result in depression either during intoxication or after the drugs leave the body, in a period known as withdrawal. The diagnosis for this disorder is made if the symptoms have begun during intoxication or withdrawal and continue afterward. The list of illicit drugs that are linked to depression is long and includes phencyclidine (PCP), cocaine, opiates, and hallucinogens such as lysergic acid diethylamide (LSD).

Alcohol, although a legal substance, is also on the list of drugs that can result in depressive symptoms. Alcohol is categorized as a depressant substance, meaning that it slows down brain activity. A person using alcohol and experiencing symptoms of depression can be diagnosed with substance/medication-induced depressive disorder. In addition, people diagnosed with other depressive disorders should consider that alcohol could make their symptoms worse. Coleman writes, "Alcohol is a central nervous system depressant that can make it harder to recover from a depressive episode."[6] Often, alcohol should not be used alongside antidepressants.

Medications prescribed for medical reasons might have depressive symptoms as side effects. For example, certain steroids, such as prednisone taken in doses higher than 80 milligrams a day, have been linked to depressive symptoms.

Oral contraceptives high in estrogen and progesterone can result in depression. One Danish study considered various methods of hormonal

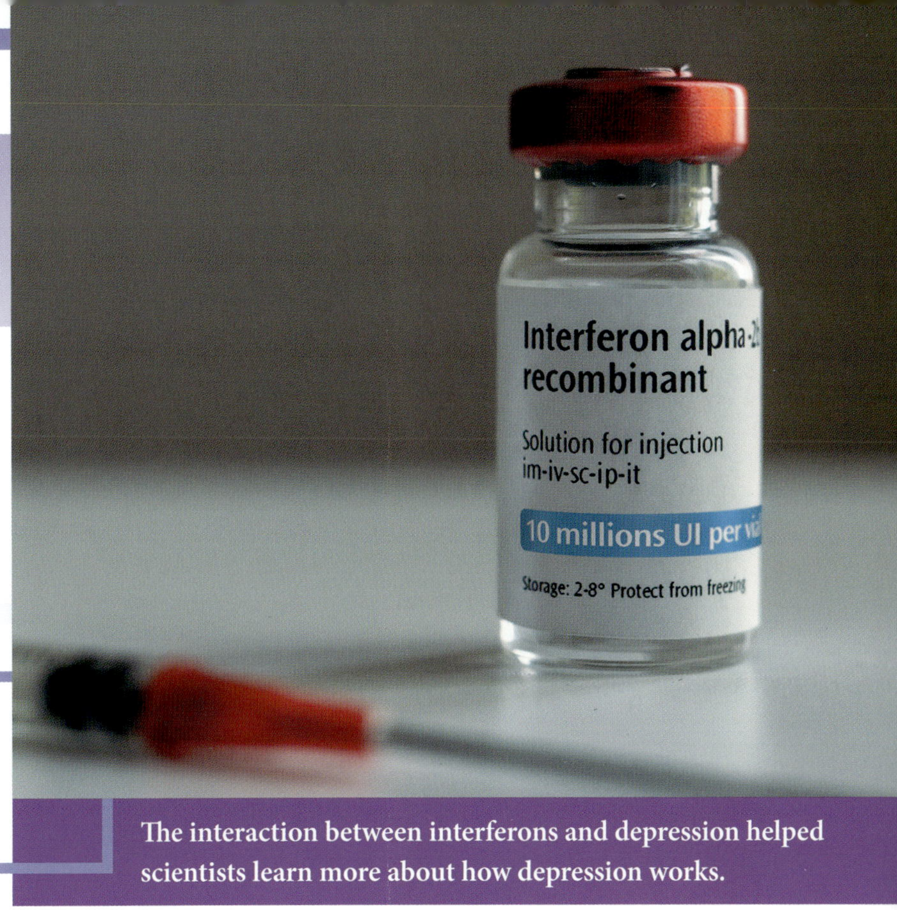

The interaction between interferons and depression helped scientists learn more about how depression works.

contraceptive use in more than one million women. The researchers found an increased risk of depression associated with hormonal contraceptive use, particularly among adolescents. Another group of researchers studied 1,236 women and their use of oral contraceptives. They concluded that adolescents who used oral contraceptives had a heightened risk of depression as adults, compared to those who began using oral contraceptives in adulthood.

Interferons are another class of medications that are known to be linked to depression. Because of

Autoimmune Diseases and Depression

Depression and autoimmune diseases frequently occur together. Autoimmune diseases happen when the body's immune system turns against its own cells. There are many autoimmune diseases, including lupus, type 1 diabetes, and rheumatoid arthritis. The connection is intriguing, but scientists are not sure why depression and autoimmune diseases are associated with one another. Perhaps autoimmune diseases cause depression, or possibly depression makes the person susceptible to autoimmune disease. Some theorize that the same underlying mechanism is at work in both depression and autoimmune disease. Additional research is needed.

the way interferons work in the body, they pointed researchers toward a new area of depression research. Interferons, manufactured proteins injected into the body as part of medical treatments, are used to treat chronic hepatitis. They fight hepatitis by sending the body's immune system into overdrive. Interferons' link to both depression and to an overactive immune system led researchers to study connections between the immune system and depression.

Depressive Disorder Due to Another Medical Condition

Depression can be caused by underlying medical issues, so the *DSM-5* has the diagnosis of depressive disorder due to another medical condition.

A person with a depressive disorder due to another medical condition must experience depressed mood and a lack of interest in activities that used to bring pleasure. One cause of this disorder can be stroke. Approximately 35 percent of people who have had a stroke become depressed.[7] Those who have strokes in the left frontal lobe are more likely to have symptoms of depression than those whose right frontal lobe is affected by the stroke. A person with traumatic brain injury may have depression as well.

Some neurodegenerative diseases, conditions in which nerve cells die, are linked to depression. Parkinson's disease and Huntington's disease are examples of such neurodegenerative diseases. The onset of depression in these diseases does not coincide with the other major symptoms of the diseases. In fact, the *DSM-5* notes that with Parkinson's disease and Huntington's disease, the depression comes before the motor and cognitive symptoms associated with each condition.

Those with forms of dementia, such as Alzheimer's disease, can also experience depression. Michelle Quilter notes specifically the well-established connection between depression and another common form of dementia, known as Lewy body disease.

Endocrine disorders, such as hypothyroidism and Cushing's disease, can have depression as a symptom as well. Hypothyroidism occurs when the thyroid gland does not produce enough of the thyroid hormone. Cushing's disease is diagnosed when the adrenal glands produce too much of the steroid hormone cortisol.

Disruptive Mood Dysregulation Disorder

Another category of depressive disorder, disruptive mood dysregulation disorder, is reserved just for children and adolescents from ages six to eighteen. A mental health professional's diagnosis is based on a pattern of consistent temper outbursts. These outbursts might be verbal or physical. A person must exhibit this irritable or angry behavior for more than a 12-month period. In any given six to 12-month period, the prevalence of people who have had this disorder is likely 2 percent to 5 percent.[8]

There are a wide variety of depressive disorders, with particular symptoms associated with each. Some of the diagnoses share much in common, but there are enough distinct features for medical professionals to distinguish between them. Within these diagnoses, these professionals can also describe particular features, known as specifiers, that can make the diagnoses more specific. A more specific description of a person's disorder may help guide his or her treatment plan.

Volunteering and Depression

Volunteering time to help others might, in turn, help a person with depression. Reaching out to others in need can give the person with depression a sense of purpose and encourage her to view herself as a valuable member of the community. Volunteering might require the person to learn and use new skills. These newly acquired skills can improve self-esteem and self-confidence. In addition, the act of socializing combats the isolation of depression. However, some people with depression may be unable to muster the energy to volunteer. Volunteering is one of many useful tools in countering mental disorders.

Chapter Four

Pinpointing a Diagnosis

The *DSM-5* includes specifiers that mental health providers can add to the diagnosis of depression. Specifiers point to particular features about the depressive disorder that should be noted in the diagnosis. The first specifier is "with anxious distress." This is used when people exhibit anxiousness in addition to their symptoms of major depressive disorder or persistent depressive disorder. They might be fearful that something terrible is going to happen to them. They can feel on edge, worried, or restless. They might even be worried that they will lose control of themselves.

Another specifier for depressive disorder is "with melancholic features." A person with this feature exhibits a constant lack of pleasure and has a mood that does not lift, even when something

Each person's case of depression is different. For some people, anxiety may appear alongside the depressive symptoms.

"Depression can't be ranked alongside adjectives like *blue, sad, dejected, down, melancholy,* or *unhappy*. Those words just won't do . . . because they don't even come close to describing what depression feels like."[1]

—Deborah Serani, author of Depression in Later Life: An Essential Guide

good happens. He might feel despair. His depression is worse in the morning. He may have a problem with waking early and not being able to get back to sleep. The person's change of eating habits is expressed in an inability to eat and a resulting weight loss.

A person diagnosed with a depressive disorder "with atypical features" will have a mood that improves when pleasant things occur. Two of the following four criteria must be met. She might overeat and gain weight. She may sleep too much and might nap in addition to having had a long night's sleep. She may complain of arms and legs that feel heavy, which is known as leaden paralysis. She might have a long-standing pattern of believing she is rejected in relationships.

A mental health professional can also diagnose an individual with depression with catatonia. People with catatonia might not move or speak at all. Some might engage in unusual physical movements. For example, they could take a physical position against gravity. In other words, they might raise their arms and leave them there. Sometimes they engage in repetitive movements, such as flapping their arms. People with catatonia might mimic what others are saying, which is called echolalia, or mimic what others are doing, which is called echopraxia.

Depressive Disorder with Psychotic Features

Depressive disorders might have the specifier of psychosis. Psychosis occurs when a person has delusions or hallucinations. Delusions are false beliefs. People with delusions hold strongly to these beliefs. They are reluctant to let go of the false beliefs even when presented with logical information that contradicts them. Matthew Griepp is the attending psychiatrist and director of fellowship training at Silver Hill Hospital in New Canaan, Connecticut. He notes that delusions in depressive disorders are typically "mood congruent." In other words, the theme of the delusions matches the person's depressed mood. Griepp explains that the individual with delusions might believe she is evil, cursed, or dying from a terrible disease. She could believe, for instance, that she is causing the suffering of people in the Middle East.

Another indication of psychosis is hallucination. Hallucinations occur when a person perceives something that does not exist in reality. He may hear, see, feel, smell, or taste things that others around him do not. As with the delusions of depressive disorders, the hallucinations in depression with psychotic features are usually consistent with the person's low mood. Griepp notes that individuals can experience auditory hallucinations, explaining that they might hear "derogatory voices telling them, 'You are no good.'"[2]

Depressive Disorder with Peripartum Onset

Depression disorder with the specifier of peripartum onset is commonly known as postpartum depression. This term suggests that it occurs after a woman gives birth. However, the term *peripartum* is used in diagnosis. This term includes the time during pregnancy as well as the time after birth. This renaming occurred because experts found that about 50 percent of major depressive episodes related to pregnancy begin during the pregnancy.[3]

A significant number of new mothers experience the symptoms of postpartum depression.

Many mothers experience what is known as baby blues in the days following the births of their babies. They might experience some depressive symptoms, such as sadness or anxiety, but the symptoms usually resolve in three to five days. Women who experience a postpartum depressive episode have more severe depressive symptoms that last longer than the baby blues. Postpartum depression usually appears within

Postpartum Depression with Psychotic Features

Approximately one in 1,000 women who give birth experience postpartum depression with psychotic features.[5] These women have delusions or hallucinations. The delusions and hallucinations often focus on the infant. The mother might, for example, have the delusion that the baby is possessed by the devil. Her hallucinations could be auditory, and she might hear voices ordering her to hurt the baby or herself. Infanticide and suicide are significant concerns with postpartum psychosis. However, treatment for this form of depression is effective, and outcomes are typically positive when mothers seek help.

a month of giving birth. One in seven women has postpartum depression.[4]

A specific cause of peripartum depression has not been determined. Experts believe it is a combination of physical, emotional, genetic, and environmental factors surrounding pregnancy. Much research into peripartum depression focuses on female hormones. During pregnancy, the hormones estrogen and progesterone are at high levels. In certain individuals, these high levels of hormones might cause changes in the brain that result in depression. In other women, the sudden drop in hormone levels after birth can trigger a depressive episode. Within a few months of giving birth, estrogen and progesterone generally return to normal levels. The levels of thyroid hormone might also drop.

Experts have identified certain risk factors for developing this type of depression. If the woman has previously been diagnosed with depression or bipolar disorder or has a family member with either of those mental illnesses, she has an increased risk. Women who have unsupportive partners and women who are under financial strain have more risk. Women who have traumatic birth experiences or have difficulty breastfeeding, mothers under 20 years of age, and those whose pregnancies were unplanned or unwanted have an elevated chance of postpartum depression.

Treatment for depressive disorder with peripartum onset may include both antidepressant medication and psychotherapy. Mental health professionals must weigh any risks that the medication could pose to the fetus or breastfeeding infant with the psychiatric needs of the mother. In March 2019, the Food and Drug Administration (FDA) approved brexanolone, the first medication specifically meant for postpartum depression. It is a steroid medication that is given intravenously for 60 hours under the supervision of a medical professional. This supervision is necessary because of the possibility of side effects. Experts advise that the medication might not be safe for pregnant or breastfeeding women.

Depressive Disorder with Seasonal Pattern

Recurrent major depressive disorder with the specifier of seasonal pattern was previously known as seasonal affective disorder (SAD). A person with the seasonal pattern specifier has the symptoms of major depressive disorder during particular seasons of the year. Most often, the symptoms begin in the autumn, continue through the winter, and fade away in the spring. However, there are some individuals who experience depressive symptoms mainly during the summer months.

People with seasonal pattern depression usually sleep too much. They often overeat and especially crave carbohydrates, such as white bread. They often withdraw from being with people and

Light Therapy

Treatments for seasonal pattern depression include antidepressant medication and psychotherapy. In addition, people with this disorder can try light therapy by using a light box. The light box simulates bright sunlight, causing the body to produce vitamin D. The individual sits close to the light box with her eyes open for a certain amount of time each day. It is important that the light box have a filter to protect the eyes from ultraviolet (UV) light.

In the United States, depression linked to seasonal changes is more common in the northern states.

> "In the fall you feel like a car that needs premium gasoline, but you have regular."[7]
>
> *—Ann West (pseudonym) speaking about her seasonal pattern depression*

have less desire to engage in activities they normally enjoy. This disorder is linked to the amount of available sunlight. It is found more often in places farther from the equator. The National Institute of Mental Health explains that the disorder affects "1 percent of those who live in Florida and 9 percent of those who live in New England or Alaska."[6] It is more prevalent in women than in men, and it is found more frequently in younger people.

Major Depressive Disorder with Mixed Features

With the "mixed features" specifier, the medical professional has found three symptoms of mania or hypomania. A person with mania has an elevated mood. Little need for sleep is a symptom of mania, as is an increase in energy. A person can display grandiosity, which means she thinks she knows better than everyone and can perform tasks better than all others. The person might behave impulsively, engaging in risky sexual actions, drug use, binge shopping, or gambling. Racing thoughts and pressured speech can be parts of mania. Pressured speech occurs when the person talks quickly without pausing. Hypomania is a less severe mania that may not reach the point where it negatively affects the person's life.

Mania and hypomania are also key features of bipolar disorders. The *DSM-5* notes that a major depressive disorder diagnosed with mixed features increases the risk that the individual will be diagnosed with bipolar I disorder or bipolar II disorder in the future.

Bipolar Disorder

Bipolar disorder is a mood disorder, just as depressive disorders are. However, the *DSM-5* does not categorize bipolar as a depressive disorder. Bipolar disorder involves alternating periods of depression and periods of mania or hypomania. A person with bipolar I disorder has depression and mania. Those with bipolar II disorder have depressive episodes and hypomania. Both medication and psychotherapy are often utilized in the treatment of bipolar disorders. Hospitalization may be required for either type of bipolar disorder.

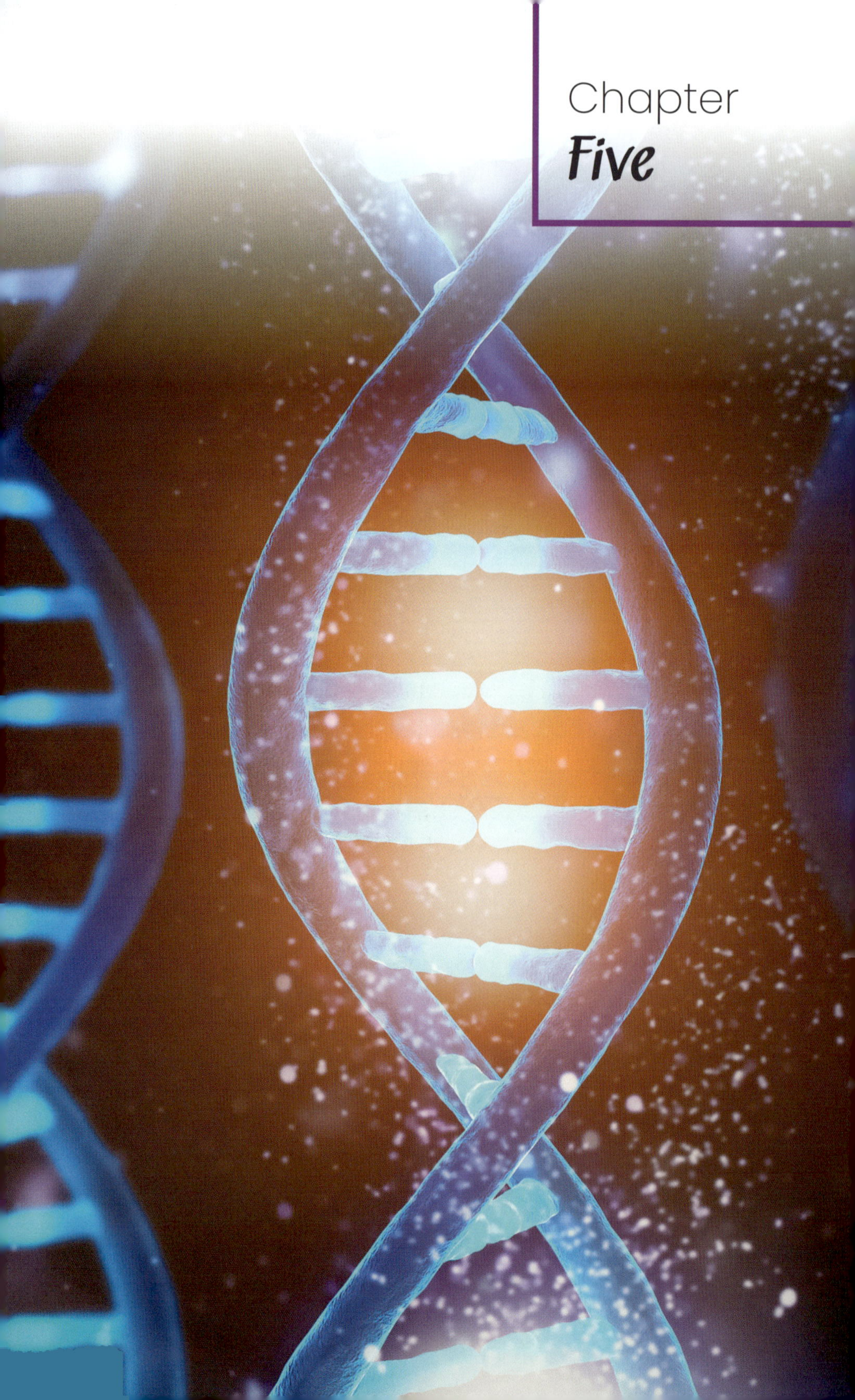

Chapter
Five

Risk Factors

Experts have not found a specific cause for depression. Instead, there are many factors that likely lead to depressive disorders. Genetic, environmental, biological, and psychological factors are all linked to depression.

Genetic Risks

Genetics are a risk factor in the development of depression. Scientists have conducted studies of twins to confirm a genetic link to depression. Identical twins share 100 percent of their genes. Fraternal twins share 50 percent of their genes. Studies have discovered that an identical twin has a much higher risk of depression if the other twin has the disorder than is the case with fraternal twins. This indicates depression has a genetic link. However, if genetics were solely responsible, identical twins would share depression 100 percent of the time, which they do not. In their large twin study, Kenneth Kendler,

Depression's genetic link has been shown by studies that analyze the disorder's presence in twins.

The History of Depression

In his article "Basic Concepts of Depression," psychiatrist Eugene S. Paykel says that melancholia was recognized as a disorder in the time of Hippocrates (approximately 460 BCE–370 BCE) in ancient Greece. At that time, the term *melancholia* referred to all types of "quiet insanity."[2] Illnesses were thought to be caused by the humors, which were black bile, yellow bile, blood, and phlegm. These substances were thought to be the fundamental components of the body and its health. Melancholia was believed to be caused by excessive black bile.

As years passed, melancholia became more closely linked with hopelessness. In the late 1800s, German psychiatrist Emil Kraepelin categorized psychiatric illnesses. He made the distinction between two categories of psychosis: dementia praecox (now called schizophrenia) and a mood category, manic-depression. Paykel writes, "The latter [Kraepelin's manic-depressive category] not only included cases of alternating mania and melancholia, but also cases of mania, and seemed to include all depressions."[3] Currently, depressive disorders are diagnosed through recognition of certain symptoms that are widely accepted by mental health professionals.

Margaret Gatz, and their colleagues concluded that major depression has a 37 percent heritability rate. That means that 37 percent of depression is likely linked to genetics, while factors other than genes are at work for the remaining 63 percent.[1]

Having a first-degree relative with depression also increases the risk that a person will be diagnosed with the disorder. First-degree relatives are siblings, parents, or children. If a first-degree relative has depression, the risk of being diagnosed is two to three times greater than for those who do not have a first-degree relative with depression. Adoption studies support this familial link. Adopted children are more likely to have depression when their biological parents have depression than adopted children whose biological parents do not have the disorder.

Environmental Risks

Genes play a significant part in developing depression, but they are not the complete story. There are other factors at work. A person's environment and experiences play a role in depression. Children who have had trauma in their lives are at greater risk for depression. A childhood trauma might mean losing a parent to death or divorce. The trauma could be having an ill parent. As another example, dealing with violence at home is a traumatic experience. Children who have experienced abuse are at greater risk for developing depression. The abuse might be physical, psychological, or sexual in nature.

A person who has experienced loss is also at higher risk for depression. The loss could be the death of a loved one. It could also be a financial loss, the loss of a job, or the end of an important relationship.

Additional Risks

Beyond genetics and environment, there are additional risks. Those with certain medical diagnoses are more likely to be diagnosed with depression. For example, a person with heart disease runs a 20 percent chance of depression.[4] A person with cancer has a 25 percent chance of depression.[5]

People with alcohol and drug use disorders are at higher risk for depression too. According to the National Alliance on Mental Illness (NAMI), "21% of adults with a substance use disorder also experienced a major depressive episode in 2018."[6] All these factors add up to create an individual's own risk profile for depression.

Neurotransmitters and Depression

Biology plays a role in depression. The brain has approximately 86 billion nerve cells called neurons. The neurons communicate with one another through electrical signals and biochemicals. Neurotransmitters are the biochemical substances that allow neurons to pass along messages.

A serious medical diagnosis, such as cancer, can leave a person more vulnerable to depression.

The neurotransmission occurs at junctions between neurons; these junctions are called synapses. There is a small gap in this area known as the synaptic cleft. The neurotransmitter travels from the sending neuron and moves across the synaptic cleft to the receiving neuron. The neurotransmitter binds with a protein receptor on the receiving neuron to complete the neuronal communication.

Researchers are studying the links of neurotransmitters to depression.

The neurotransmitters serotonin, norepinephrine, and dopamine have been the focus of much depression research, but recently glutamate has been studied as well. Each neurotransmitter has particular jobs to do. Serotonin regulates sleep, appetite, and mood. Norepinephrine is connected to stress, sleep, attention, and focus. Dopamine has a role in reward, emotion, learning, and motor control. Glutamate affects synaptic plasticity. Plasticity is the name for the brain's ability to form new neural pathways. Many treatments for depression attempt to increase and stabilize the amount of those neurotransmitters available in the brain.

Brain Differences

Scientists have noted differences in the brains of those diagnosed with depression when compared to those of healthy individuals. They are able to look at the brain with the use of technology. They use positron emission tomography (PET) scans, single photon emission computed tomography (SPECT) scans, MRI scans, and functional MRI (fMRI) scans. Many of the brain differences found in depression are centered in the brain's limbic system, specifically in the amygdala and hippocampus. The amygdala is a portion of the brain responsible for

Descartes Dualism

René Descartes was a French philosopher and mathematician who lived in the 1600s. He theorized that there was an outer physical world and an inner spiritual world. The body belonged to the physical realm, and the mind belonged to the spiritual realm. This concept, known as dualism, persists in modern society. The body and mind, or psyche, are viewed as separate.

In his book, *The Inflamed Mind: A Radical New Approach to Depression*, Edward Bullmore writes about how this separation divides medical and psychological care in the United Kingdom. He says, "Patients literally go through different doors, attend different hospitals, to consult differently trained doctors, about their dualistically divided bodies and minds."[7] However, modern studies of mental illness, such as depression, are finding many biological links to mental disorders. These links bring the stark division between body and mind into question. Some scholars argue that the idea of a split between body and mind may have led to stigma toward those with mental disorders.

emotions, including fear, happiness, and sadness. The hippocampus is involved in emotional memory.

Many studies have revealed a reduced hippocampal volume in the brains of those with depression as compared to the hippocampal volume of healthy individuals. In an experiment, Ronny Redlich, Nils Opel, and colleagues compared the brains of 20 adolescents diagnosed with depression and 20 healthy adolescents using both fMRIs and structural MRIs. They found the hippocampal volumes of the adolescents with depression were smaller compared to the hippocampal volumes of the healthy adolescents.

In their study, the researchers also made a connection between reduced hippocampal volume and childhood abuse. Both depressed adolescents and healthy adolescents who had undergone abuse in childhood had reduced hippocampal volume when compared to those without histories of abuse. This difference might be explained by studies that link childhood trauma to increased exposure to stress hormones. Research suggests that, over time, this exposure to stress hormones can slow the growth of neurons in the hippocampus.

Several studies have shown that the amygdala is more active when subjects with depression are exposed to negative emotional stimuli, compared to the amygdalae of people without depression. In their experiment, Redlich and colleagues showed photos of faces with different emotions to their subjects. They found that the amygdalae of the adolescents with depression were overly active when presented with facial photos that showed negative emotions. The amygdalae of the healthy group did not demonstrate the same type of activity.

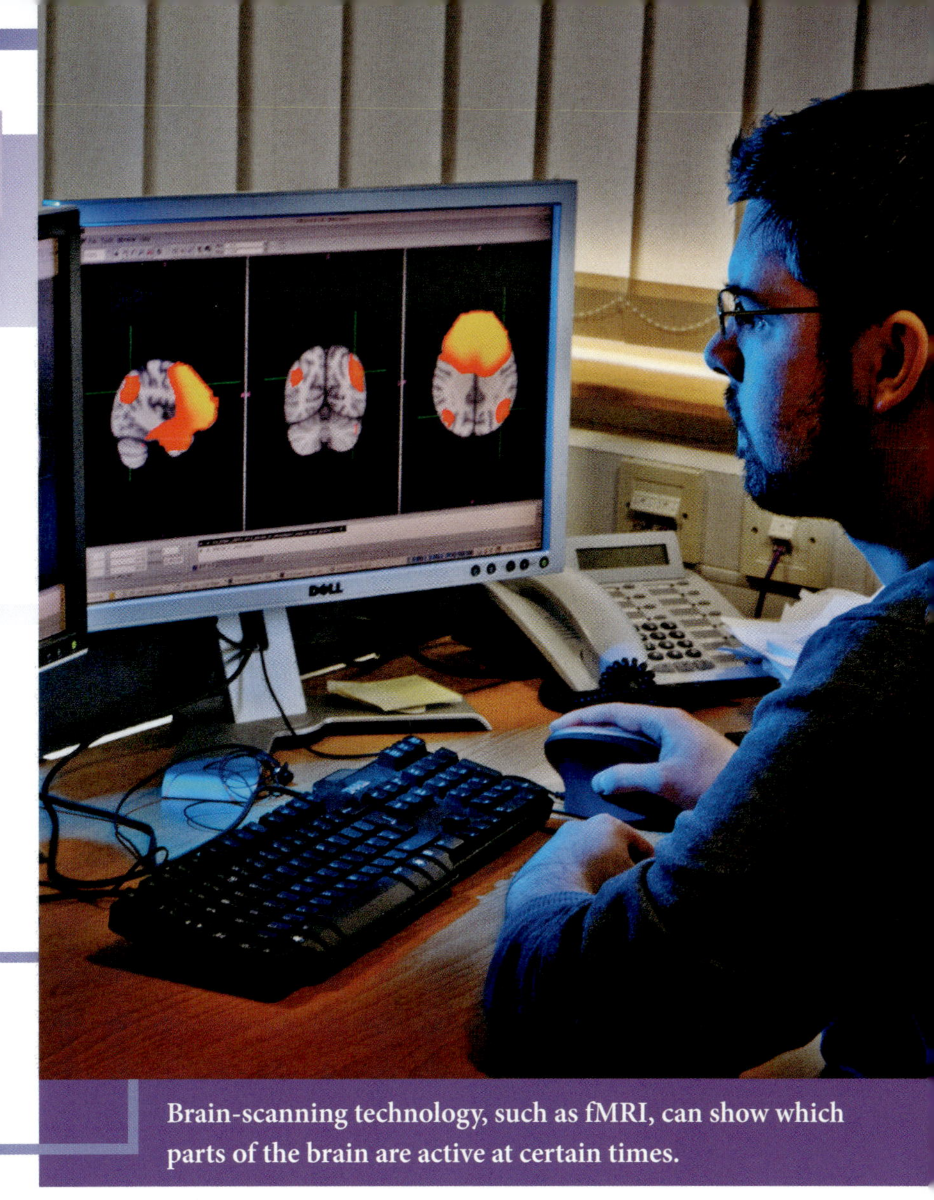

Brain-scanning technology, such as fMRI, can show which parts of the brain are active at certain times.

Researchers are also exploring a possible association between the anterior cingulate cortex (ACC) and depression. The ACC links the limbic system to the prefrontal cortex. This is the part of the brain responsible for cognitive functions.

Suicide Risk

Another common symptom of depression is having suicidal ideation or taking suicidal actions. Some people with depression might think about death, but they might not have concrete plans to end their lives. For example, they could be hoping to die passively in their sleep. Other people think more seriously about actually taking their own lives. Some individuals have particular plans in place for ending their lives. They may have chosen a time, method, and place. Some people eventually act on taking their own lives.

Certain groups of people are more at risk of suicide than others. More women than men attempt to kill themselves. However, more men than women end up dying by suicide. American Indians and Alaskan Natives have the highest rate of suicide.

There are risk factors that make an individual more likely to be suicidal. A person is at risk if she has depression or another mental illness, or if she has family members with mental illness. Those with substance use problems or with family members with substance use issues are also at increased risk. Someone who has suffered a loss in her life is at higher risk. The loss could be the death of a loved one, job loss, financial loss, or a loss of a relationship, as in a divorce.

Suicide risk is higher for an individual who has attempted suicide before or has a family history of suicide. A person could also be at risk if he is exposed to the suicide or suicidal behavior of a friend or family member, a person in the community, or a celebrity. The risk of suicide is greater if there are guns or if the individual is exposed to violence in the home. According to the National Institute of Mental Health, "being between the ages of 15 and 24 or over age 60" is also a risk factor for suicide.[8] Finally, there is more of a risk for people who have been to jail or who have certain physical illnesses.

Signs of Suicide

A person considering suicide may or may not display obvious signs. The individual could talk about death or ending his life. He might isolate himself from people. Increasing his intake of alcohol or using drugs can be a sign. He could gather the means necessary to kill himself, such as amassing pills or purchasing a gun. He might put his affairs in order. For example, he might write a will or give prized possessions away. The person could offer final words of love and say goodbye to family and friends. In some people, however, there are no outward signs of suicidality.

Quilter explains how a depressive disorder is a risk for suicide. A person might consider suicide because she wants to end her pain and she has no hope that things will change. Other people think about suicide because they see themselves as burdens to family and friends. These ways of thinking—the lack of hope and negative self-view—are both symptoms of depression. Once the disorder and its symptoms are treated, thoughts of suicide usually disappear.

There Is Help

If a person feels suicidal, Griepp advises, "Get yourself evaluated."[9] Go somewhere safe, such as a hospital emergency room, or contact a mental health professional. The National Suicide Prevention Hotline is there to help too. Its phone number is 1-800-273-8255, and it can be reached at its website, suicidepreventionlifeline.org, as well. After suicide, Griepp says, there is no second chance.

> "Being suicidal is not a rational state of mind. If treated, they will see things differently."[10]
>
> *—Matthew Griepp, MD, attending psychiatrist at Silver Hill Hospital*

Griepp offers similar advice to friends or family of a person who experiences suicidal ideation. They can encourage the person to get somewhere safe and speak to a professional. Family members and friends should not be the ones to decide whether the person is really going to kill himself. They are not qualified to make that determination.

Quilter expands on this by saying that friends and family members are likely to approach the individual too subjectively. They don't want to accept that the person they love would truly end his life. In addition, the suicidal individual might be reluctant to tell the truth about his plans because he doesn't want to hurt his family members' feelings. Griepp also notes that if a person calls and says he is suicidal, it is important to make sure he hasn't already taken some action, such as swallowing pills. If suicidal action has been taken, this will require an emergency call for an ambulance.

It is a myth that asking a person whether she is suicidal will put ideas in her head. Knowing that an individual has suicidal thoughts is a path to finding the proper help. In addition, it is never a good idea to assume that someone threatening suicide is doing it for attention. A person thinking and talking about suicide should be taken seriously.

Chapter Six

Current Treatments

Major depressive disorder may resolve on its own within a year, but before then a person could lose her job, her relationships, or possibly her life. In addition, major depression recurs in 50 percent of people within a year and 85 percent of people in their lifetimes.[1] It is important to know that there are effective treatments available for depressive disorders. Antidepressant medication, psychotherapy, and brain stimulation therapies have proven successful in the treatment of depressive symptoms.

Antidepressant Medications

Experts believe that there is a connection between certain neurotransmitters in the brain and depression. Most antidepressant medication works to increase the availability of these neurotransmitters. The medications target serotonin, norepinephrine,

For many people, antidepressant medication is a highly effective treatment for depression.

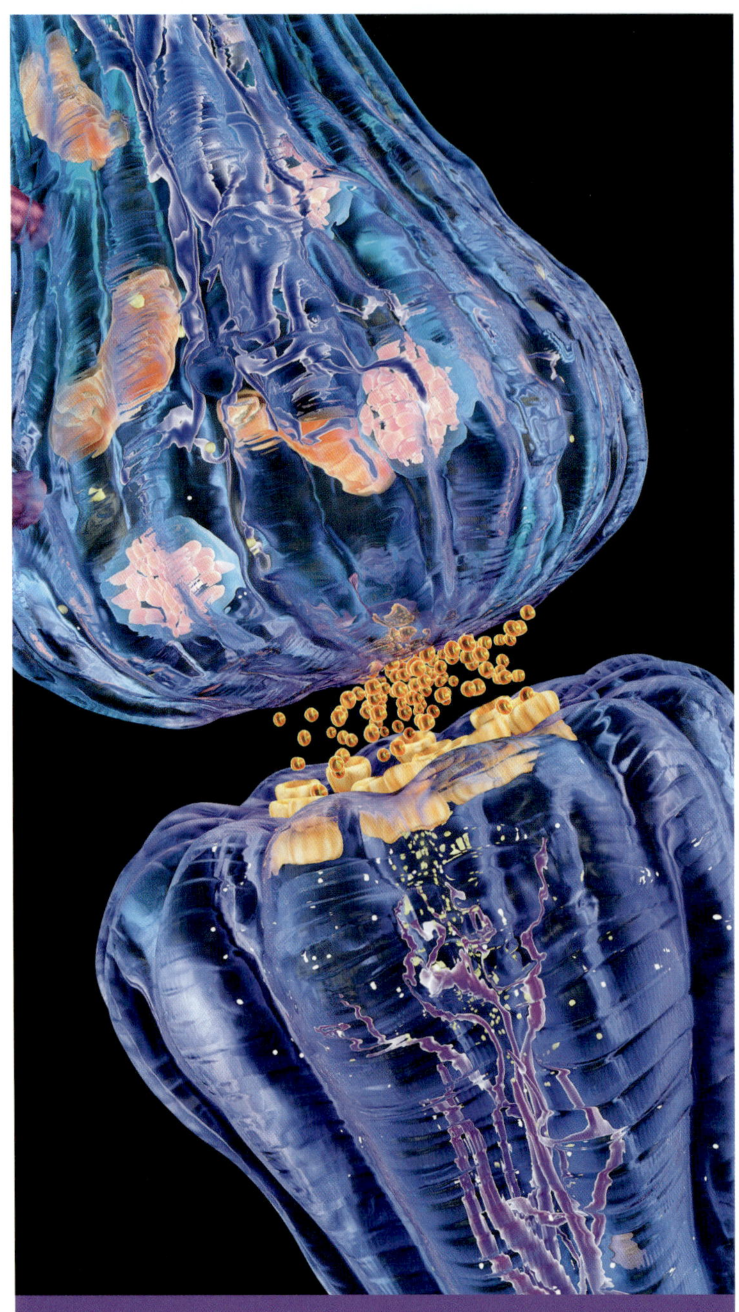

Many antidepressants affect chemicals that work at the synaptic cleft, the space where two neurons meet.

and dopamine, or a combination of these. The mechanism by which the antidepressants work varies, but they all increase and stabilize the available levels of certain neurotransmitters.

In the 1980s, researchers found that selective serotonin reuptake inhibitors (SSRIs) relieved depressive symptoms. SSRIs, such as fluoxetine (Prozac) or paroxetine (Paxil), specifically target the neurotransmitter serotonin. The sending neuron releases serotonin into the synaptic cleft. The serotonin attaches to the receptors of the receiving neuron. After communication, the serotonin is released back into the synaptic cleft to be reabsorbed by the sending neuron. This reabsorption is known as reuptake. SSRIs inhibit the reuptake of serotonin, leaving more of it available in the synaptic cleft. This extra serotonin can continue to bind with the receiving neuron.

Serotonin-norepinephrine reuptake inhibitors (SNRIs) work by a similar mechanism as SSRIs do. However, they inhibit both serotonin and norepinephrine reuptake. Available SNRIs include duloxetine (Cymbalta) and venlafaxine (Effexor XR).

Tricyclic antidepressants (TCAs) have been available since the 1950s. They include amitriptyline

(Elavil) and imipramine (Tofranil). Tricyclic medications primarily inhibit the reuptake of serotonin and norepinephrine, though they do so in a different way than SNRIs.

Beginning in the 1950s, monoamine oxidase inhibitors (MAOIs) were also used to treat depression. MAOIs inhibit the activity of the enzyme monoamine oxidase. Monoamine oxidase is responsible for breaking down the neurotransmitters serotonin, norepinephrine, and dopamine. MAOIs stop the enzyme from breaking down these neurotransmitters and leave more of them active in the brain. Phenelzine (Nardil) and tranylcypromine (Parnate) are examples of MAOIs.

There are also atypical antidepressants. These work a bit differently than the other categories. For instance, bupropion (Wellbutrin) works by inhibiting the reuptake of the neurotransmitters dopamine and norepinephrine, but it is chemically unique compared to the antidepressants from the major categories. Mirtazapine (Remeron) and trazodone (Desyrel) are two other effective antidepressants that have a slightly different mechanism than other antidepressants.

The more recent antidepressants, SSRIs and SNRIs, are prescribed more often than the older

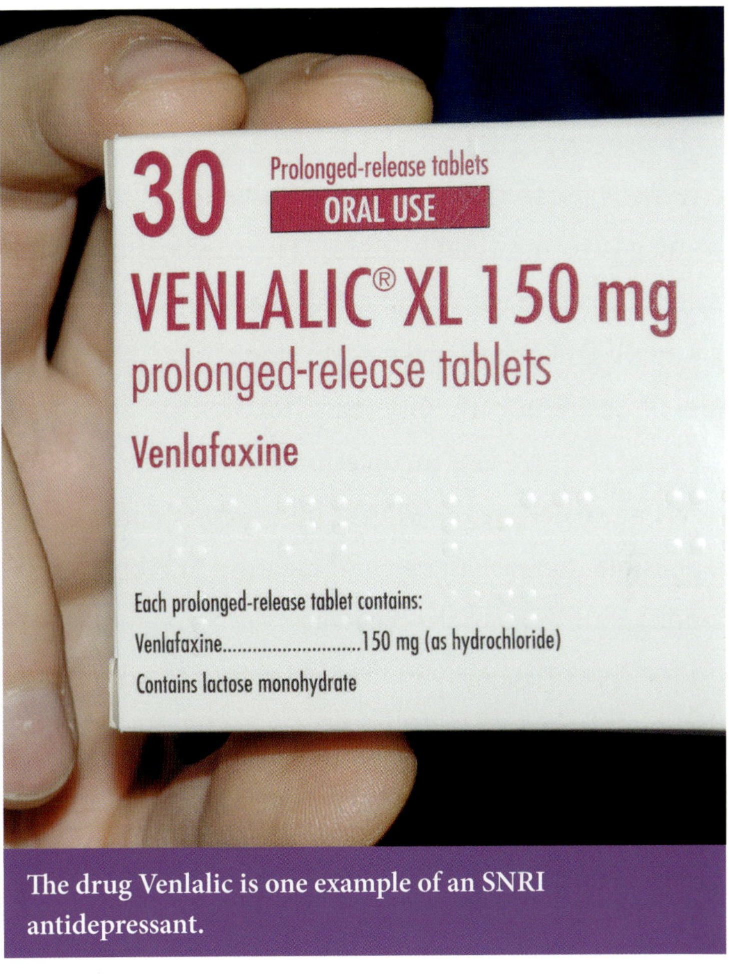

The drug Venlalic is one example of an SNRI antidepressant.

antidepressants, TCAs and MAOIs. The older antidepressants are no more effective than the newer ones, and they can have more serious side effects. According to NAMI, "MAOIs are the least prescribed of antidepressants because they can cause dangerously high blood pressure when combined with certain foods and medications."[2] People taking

MAOIs must avoid certain foods, such as sauerkraut and aged cheese.

However, SSRIs and SNRIs can also have side effects. A person taking these medications can have some gastrointestinal troubles. The medications might interfere with eating and sleeping habits. Some people experience sexual side effects, such as loss of desire or difficulty reaching orgasm. Since 2004, antidepressant medications have carried a warning issued by the FDA. The warning addresses a possible increase in suicidal ideation and behavior among children, adolescents, and young adults under 25, particularly in the first weeks of taking the medication.

Today's researchers are questioning exactly how these antidepressant medications work to help people with depression feel better. Scientists believe that depression is linked to low levels of certain neurotransmitters, but they are unsure why, when the levels are increased by the medications, it may take weeks for the person to feel better. One theory is that these medications work because they affect neurogenesis. Neurogenesis is the growth of new neurons, and it takes time.

Psychiatrists are typically able to prescribe medication for patients with depression.

Prescribing Antidepressants

Mental health professionals understand that prescribing antidepressant medication often involves some trial and error. Griepp says, "There's not a great way to predict which medication will be effective with which patient."[3] There are many antidepressants from which to choose. If one medication does not work for a person, it is not the fault of the patient, and others can be tried. Mental health professionals strive to find the most effective medication with the least number of side effects for the patient.

Most mental health professionals prescribe the newer medications, such as SSRIs and SNRIs, first because they have fewer side effects than the older medications. Mental health specialists consider several variables when prescribing antidepressants. For example, if the patient has anxiety in addition to depression, they might look for a medication known to address both. They also consider what other medications the patient is taking so that there won't be any worrisome interactions.

Prescribers take care to be mindful of the potential side effects of medications. They work closely with the needs of their patients. If a patient is diabetic or concerned about gaining weight, they might avoid prescribing medications, such as Remeron, that have increased appetite or weight gain as side effects. On the other hand, if a patient is a frail person who is losing weight, the mental health professional might choose that very medication to prescribe. Similarly, if a patient is having trouble sleeping, a prescriber might choose an antidepressant with sedative properties, such as Trazodone. However, if the patient sleeps too much, this same medication would be counterproductive. Some medications stay in the body longer. Prescribers might select these types of medication for someone who has trouble remembering to take medication.

Doctors will often adjust the dose of the patient's medication slowly. They might also add another medication to boost the effectiveness of the original one. Antidepressants can take six to eight weeks to be fully effective. The patient might notice certain symptoms improving, such as difficulties with sleep and eating, before realizing a lift in mood.

Psychotherapy

Psychotherapy and medication are effective treatment options for depressive disorders. There are many types of psychotherapy from which to choose. Griepp says that the most important factor in the success of any psychotherapy is having "a good rapport with the therapist."[4] The client should

> "Studies suggest that for treating depression, a short-term, goal oriented approach often is the most successful."[5]
>
> *—Keith Kramlinger, MD, editor in chief, Mayo Clinic on Depression*

> "Focusing outward on other people is the most important thing you can do if you're depressed."[7]
>
> *—Philip Burguières, mental health advocate, speaking about his recovery from depression*

feel understood by the therapist. In addition, the client should believe that they share common goals for the therapy's outcome.

Experts have found that cognitive behavioral therapy (CBT) is a particularly effective therapy choice for those with depression. CBT is a short-term talk therapy. In CBT, the client and therapist work closely together in a collaborative way. CBT gives the client concrete coping skills to deal with her depression. In CBT, the client is challenged to understand how her thoughts, actions, and emotions are linked. The concept of the therapy is that if a client learns to make a change in one of these categories, the others will change as well.

Dialectical behavioral therapy (DBT) is a specific type of CBT. Quilter says, "DBT was first used with suicidal, depressed females in the '80s and found to be successful." One of the essential differences between DBT and CBT, Quilter says, is that "DBT encourages the client to be present with an emotion rather than blocking it out."[6] Quilter says that DBT begins by accepting whatever the client is feeling and goes from there. It is a blend of tolerating distress and making changes.

DBT offers people group therapy sessions, individual therapy, and 24-hour phone coaching. DBT therapists should belong to consultation teams, which are comprised of other DBT specialists. In this way, the therapist has the advantage of consulting with a group of experts about the client's therapy.

"A big part of DBT is generating hope for life," Quilter says. The client identifies what makes life worth living and sets goals from there. The client learns concrete skills and is given workbook assignments, as well as assignments to put the skills into action. For example, one of the skills is opposite action. If a client feels sad and doesn't want to get out of bed, he accepts that present emotion. Then, he makes a cognitive decision to act in an opposite manner. He leaves the bed. Quilter says, "By acknowledging the emotion urge and acting opposite of that emotion urge, the client can stop engaging in ineffective behaviors."[8]

Mindfulness is an important concept in DBT. An individual practicing mindfulness is not worrying about the future or preoccupied by the past. The person concentrates on what he experiences with

ECT has been shown to be an effective treatment for depression that is resistant to other forms of treatment.

his senses. If he is walking outside, he listens to the birds and watches the trees sway in the breeze. He is mindful of his breathing. Mindfulness can be active, like walking, or it may take the form of a meditation practice.

Brain Stimulation Therapies

There are additional therapy options beyond medication and talk therapy. Some of these therapies attempt to stimulate the brain to relieve the symptoms of depression. Electroconvulsive therapy (ECT) is one type of brain stimulation technique. For ECT, the patient is anesthetized and given muscle relaxants. Electrodes are placed on the patient's head, and an electrical current is passed into the brain. The electrical current causes a seizure. The patient has treatments two to three times weekly for three

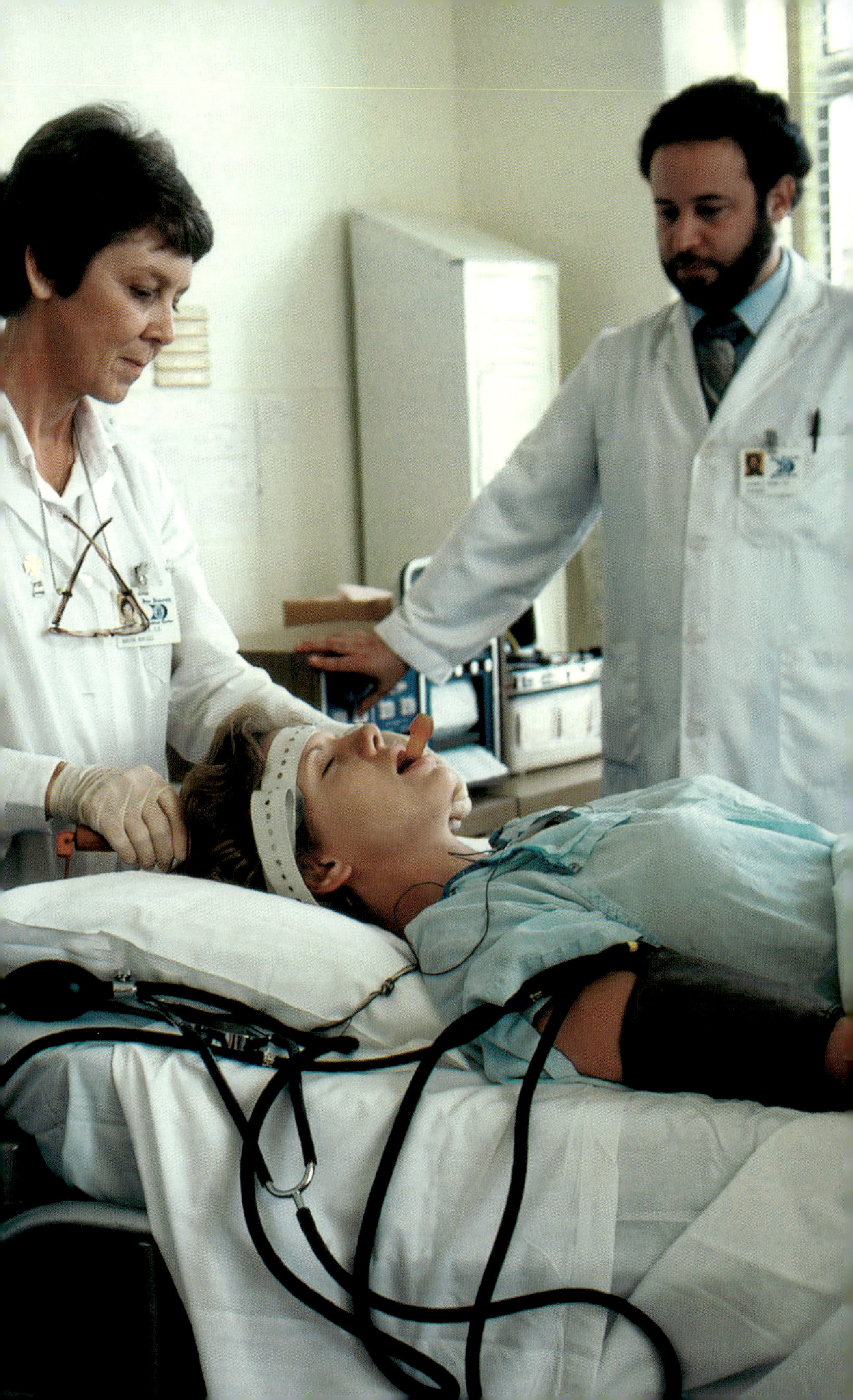

to four weeks. The exact mechanism of how ECT works is unclear. The Mayo Clinic, a leading US hospital, notes that it "seems to cause changes in brain chemistry that can quickly reverse symptoms of certain mental health conditions."[9]

Griepp says, "ECT is probably the best antidepressant treatment we've got, but it suffers terribly from stigma."[10] ECT was portrayed in a frightening way in movies such as *One Flew Over the Cuckoo's Nest*. With its controversial reputation and with the advent of antidepressant medication, ECT fell out of favor for decades.

Griepp notes that ECT is particularly useful with suicidal patients and those with psychosis.

Repetitive Transcranial Magnetic Stimulation

Repetitive transcranial magnetic stimulation (rTMS) is a brain stimulation technique used in cases of treatment-resistant depression. No anesthetic is required for this procedure. An electromagnetic coil is placed on the patient's head close to the area of the brain involved in mood, and electromagnetic pulses are passed into the brain. rTMS is given as a series of treatments. In a 2010 study by the National Institute of Mental Health, 30 percent of patients achieved remission from their depression.[11] Researchers continue to study the effectiveness of rTMS as a depression treatment.

These patients need to improve quickly and cannot wait the weeks it often takes for antidepressant medication to take effect. ECT is also used with patients who have treatment-resistant depression, which is when antidepressant medications and therapy have not worked.

ECT can cause some memory loss. More recent memories are at a greater risk of being lost than those formed long before ECT. ECT can be given bilaterally, meaning on both sides of the head, or unilaterally, meaning on one side of the head. According to the National Institute of Mental Health, "In unilateral ECT, the electrodes are placed on just one side of the head—typically the right side because it is opposite the brain's learning and memory areas."[12] Doctors and patients often choose unilateral ECT because it is less likely to cause memory loss.

Vagus Nerve Stimulation

Vagus nerve stimulation (VNS) is sometimes used for treatment-resistant depression. VNS begins with the surgical implantation of a device into the chest. The device is attached to the left vagus nerve. This nerve takes messages to the brain. The device sends intermittent electrical pulses to the left vagus nerve. Experts think this stimulation affects particular neurotransmitters in the brain that help improve mood. Further study is needed to test exactly how effective this treatment is.

Chapter *Seven*

Living with Depression

People diagnosed with depressive disorders face challenges every day. However, with the proper treatment, they can significantly reduce persistent sadness and the other difficult symptoms of depression. These people can have lives filled with triumphs and successes.

A Case of Major Depression

May Wolfe, a woman using a pseudonym, was diagnosed with major depression in her late teens. She remembers changes in her life beginning around 13 years of age. Wolfe experienced typical symptoms of major depression, including a change in eating habits and a loss of pleasure and motivation. She began to overeat. She didn't want to go out with friends on the weekends. Some days, she wasn't motivated to get out of bed or take a shower.

Depression generally affects all parts of a person's daily life, but with treatment those struggles can be eased.

Self-Injury

Psychologist Deborah Serani wrote an article called "Depression and Non-Suicidal Self Injury: When Skin Becomes an Emotional Canvas." In the article, she discusses nonsuicidal self-injury (NSSI), such as cutting or scratching. This is an unhealthy behavior that should always be taken seriously. She says that people who engage in NSSI hurt themselves physically to release emotional pain. Serani writes, "It's important to note that self-injury does not involve a conscious intent to commit suicide."[3]

When Wolfe was a freshman in high school, she started cutting herself. She says that the cutting was not suicidal behavior. She just didn't know how to handle her emotions. Wolfe says, "What I was feeling was too big to deal with. I took it out on myself."[1]

Wolfe was a junior in high school when someone called the school and mistakenly reported she was suicidal. She wasn't feeling suicidal, but that call paved the way for her to find professional help. Wolfe found a licensed clinical social worker with whom she felt comfortable. Wolfe felt the social worker was nurturing. She says, "She had a maternal vibe."[2] Experts advise that people should feel at ease and trust their therapists to achieve positive results.

Trauma

Those who experienced trauma in their childhoods are at risk for depression. Wolfe had trauma in her childhood. Her great-uncle sexually molested her. Her mother was diagnosed with psychosis when Wolfe was only seven years old. Her mother's mental illness caused her mother to act unpredictably. Her mom required hospitalizations that took her away from the family. Not only did Wolfe miss her mother but she also had to step in to care for her younger sibling.

Some people with depression consider suicide. There were times when Wolfe thought about ending her life. However, she never had a concrete plan. "I didn't want to die," says Wolfe. "I wanted the pain to go away." Still, Wolfe resisted taking antidepressant medication for more than ten years. "I thought if I went on medication, I would be like my mom," Wolfe says.[4]

Everyday Challenges

Depression can interfere substantially with career and school. In high school and college, Wolfe's fatigue and cognitive symptoms got in the way of doing her work. Wolfe recalls, "It took me so much energy to focus

Seeking support from friends is one way to help manage depression.

on schoolwork. Even to take schoolbooks out and to organize, I would be so tired from that. I couldn't even remember what I'd read in the textbooks."[5]

A general lack of interest and motivation are common symptoms of depression. Either hypersomnia, an excess of sleeping, or insomnia, a difficulty sleeping, can be present too. Some days, Wolfe's hypersomnia had her sleeping into the afternoon. When she was awake, she struggled with doing the simplest of tasks. During one such period, Wolfe says, "Even putting chicken on a plate and into the toaster oven was overwhelming."[6]

Depression can also cause a person to experience low self-esteem. Compounding this problem, the stigma of mental illness can be a stumbling block for those with depression. Sometimes a person's friends and relatives may not properly understand mental illness. They may not grasp the difficulties depressive symptoms can cause. Wolfe notes that her own relatives frequently view her depression as a personal weakness. They have a "pick yourself up by your bootstraps" mindset, she says. One told her, "I don't think you try hard enough."[7]

Treatment Successes

With time, Wolfe chose to see a psychiatrist. He prescribed her the antidepressant medication fluoxetine (Prozac) and eventually augmented

Get Solid Sleep

Nurse practitioner Judith Beck recommends that her patients with depression get good, solid sleep. She suggests seven to eight hours a night with a consistent bedtime. "No staying up past midnight," she says.[8] Getting sunshine during the day can help with setting a regular sleep schedule.

The National Sleep Foundation also stresses the importance of sleep in staying healthy. It says sleep "can heavily influence your outlook on life, energy level, motivation, and emotions."[9] To improve sleep, the organization recommends getting out in the sun, avoiding naps, and reducing the intake of alcohol and caffeine.

that with a small dose of bupropion (Wellbutrin). NAMI notes that antidepressant medication coupled with psychotherapy provides the best outcomes for most people. Wolfe felt this combined treatment approach worked well for her. She says, "With just pills, you're not examining any issues."[10]

Healthy Eating

A person with depression should eat a healthful diet. Nurse practitioner Judith Beck suggests a balanced selection of foods, including plenty of fresh fruits and vegetables when available. She recommends adding fish, such as sardines, to the diet. They are rich in omega-3 fatty acids. Omega-3 fatty acids are being studied to determine whether they might help with depression.

CBT and DBT are forms of therapy often recommended for depression. DBT emphasizes mindfulness. Mindfulness can keep a person focused on the present moment. The opposite action skill emphasized in DBT can also be helpful to some people with depression. If a person feels overwhelmed by the prospect of cleaning her living room, for example, she accepts that feeling but then cleans the room. With DBT therapy, Wolfe's condition improved. Once a person finds a combination of treatments that works, it is important to maintain it diligently.

A Case of Depressive Disorder with Seasonal Pattern

Ann West, a woman using a pseudonym, was married to a military officer. She and her husband had two young children when he was assigned to a military post near Fairbanks, Alaska. Depressive disorder with seasonal pattern occurs more often at higher latitudes. When Thanksgiving comes around at the end of November, this area of the country has only about one hour of sunlight each day.

During that time, West noticed a depressed mood and low energy. West said, "I could sense the sun pulling away, and with it, a pulling away of my energy."[11] She wanted to sleep all the time. Low mood, low energy, and hypersomnia are all typical symptoms of depressive disorder with seasonal pattern.

Daily Challenges

Depression with the seasonal pattern specifier can interfere with family relationships and with work. West experienced these difficulties. She had time off from her job for the month of December. She was excited to have the opportunity to plan a happy and memorable Christmas for her children. However, in the dark Alaskan winter, things didn't go as she had hoped. West was fatigued and got very little done each day. Her need for sleep had her crawling back into bed by four o'clock in the afternoon.

West was eventually diagnosed with seasonal affective disorder (SAD), which is now called major depressive disorder with seasonal pattern. She was relieved to have the diagnosis. She says, "Knowing what was happening really helped."[12] Looking back, she realizes that she probably had the disorder since she was a teen. She remembers her mood dropping and her energy leaving her in the autumn and winter. Then, in the spring and summer, her mood lifted and she was more productive.

Exercise and Depression

Those with depression can take self-help steps to relieve their symptoms. Experts recommend regular exercise, consistent sleep, and a healthy diet to cope with depression. West follows this advice as she manages her depression. She spends as much time as she can out walking in the sunshine.

Exercise is useful for depression because it results in brain changes and improved sleep quality. Those brain changes might be connected to endorphins the body releases during exercise. Endorphins are

Regular exercise, already important for maintaining physical health, can help with the symptoms of depression too.

chemicals that elevate mood. Consistent low-intensity exercise can also encourage the growth of neurons and new neural connections. Dr. Michael Craig Miller says, "Exercise supports nerve growth in the hippocampus, improving nerve cell connections, which helps relieve depression."[13]

Miller says exercise can be a highly effective treatment. He says, "For some people, [exercise] works as well as antidepressants, although exercise alone is not enough for someone with severe depression."[14] It is important for a person to choose an exercise activity she enjoys. This will ensure that she will continue to exercise consistently.

Chapter *Eight*

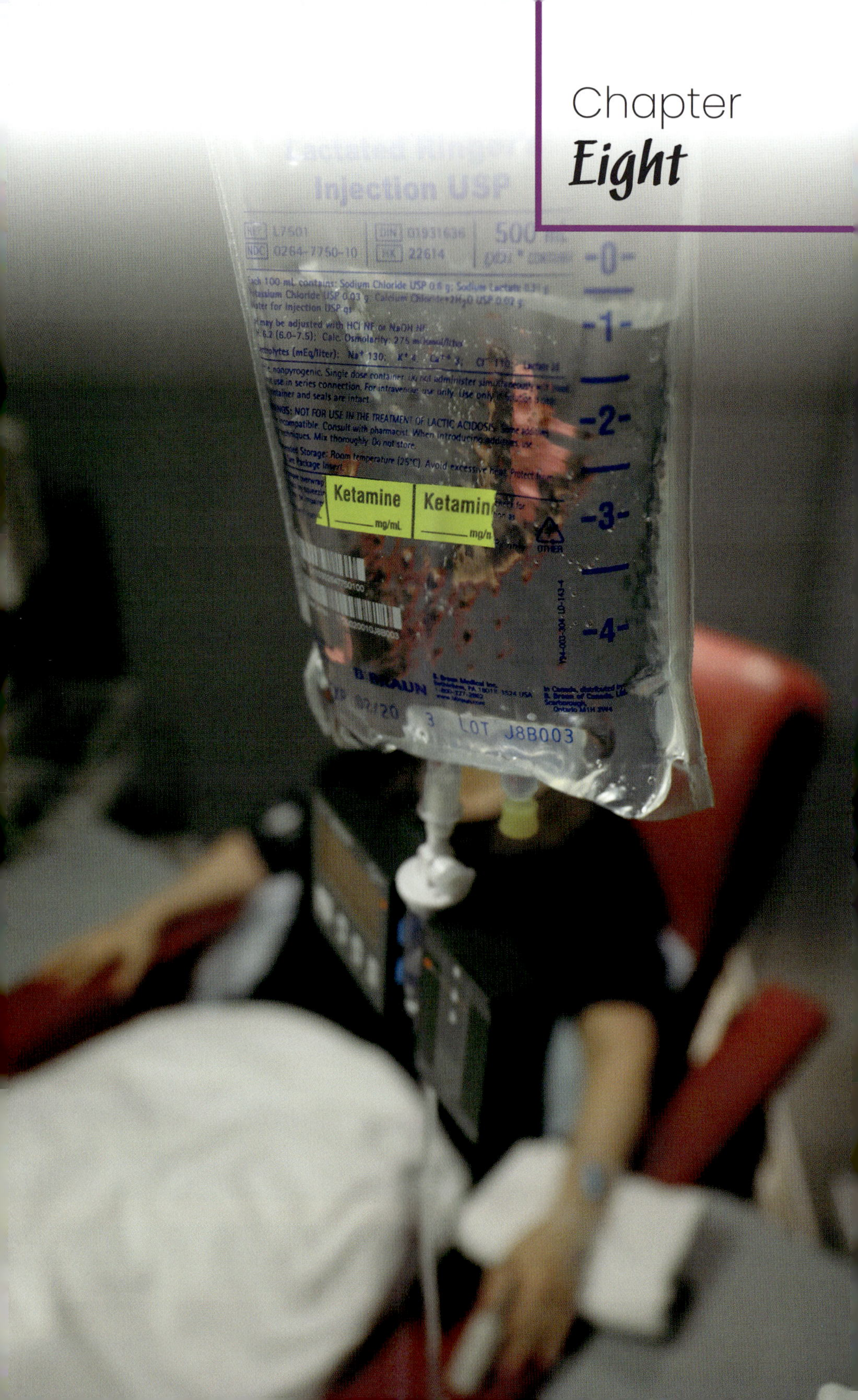

Treatments on the Horizon

Effective treatments for depressive disorders exist. In addition, scientists are doing research to discover new treatments. Researchers are exploring treatments including ketamine, anti-inflammatory drugs, and deep brain stimulation.

Ketamine

Ketamine is an anesthetic. In the 1990s, Yale University researchers discovered that ketamine offered relief to those with chronic depressive symptoms. Further research has shown that ketamine works to turn off N-methyl-D-aspartate (NMDA) receptors in the brain. This allows more of the neurotransmitter glutamate to remain in the synaptic cleft. Previously, the neurotransmitters serotonin, norepinephrine, and dopamine had been the focus of depression research.

A patient receives ketamine treatment for depression at a Chicago, Illinois, clinic in 2018.

According to Dr. Robert C. Meisner, ketamine also activates receptors known as the AMPA receptors. Meisner writes, "Together, the initial blockade of the NMDA receptors and activation of AMPA receptors lead to the release of other molecules that help neurons communicate with each other along new pathways. Known as synaptogenesis, this process likely affects mood, thought patterns, and cognition."[1] In his recent research, Griepp finds that these new or improved pathways formed through ketamine treatment can be useful to the patient as she participates in subsequent CBT.

The quick action of ketamine makes it a viable option for patients who are suicidal. The ketamine treatment is usually given intravenously two to three times in a week. The treatment might need to be maintained because ketamine's effects diminish. In 2019, a nasal spray called esketamine (Spravato) was approved by the FDA as a treatment for treatment-resistant depression.

Psilocybin

Psilocybin is a psychedelic substance found naturally in the psilocybe family of mushrooms. Studies have indicated that psilocybin can improve depressive symptoms in those with depressive disorder.

In one research study, Robin Carhart-Harris, Leor Roseman, and their colleagues administered two doses of psilocybin to each of 19 patients with treatment-resistant depression. One week after treatment, all 19 patients showed a reduction in depressive symptoms. The researchers note that the effect of psilocybin was "rapid and sustained."[2]

The relief of depressive symptoms is likely connected to the intoxication experience of psilocybin. In another study, Carhart-Harris, M. Bolstridge, and their colleagues write, "Reduction

Some researchers have explored the antidepressant potential of psilocybin, a substance found in certain mushrooms. Psilocybin is sometimes used illegally as a recreational drug.

in depressive symptoms at 5 weeks were predicted by the quality of the acute psychedelic experience."[3] In other words, a powerful experience with these specific mushrooms was linked to improvement in the depressive symptoms. Clinical trials are being done to further test the effectiveness of psilocybin in the treatment of depression.

The Immune System

Scientists are investigating how the human immune system might be connected to depression. In psychiatrist Edward Bullmore's book *The Inflamed Mind: A Radical New Approach to Depression*, he discusses this connection. Bullmore begins by

Other Treatments

S-Adenosyl-L-Methionine (SAMe) is a naturally occurring chemical in the body. Some people take SAMe as a supplement to treat depressive symptoms. According to the National Center for Complementary and Integrative Health, some studies demonstrate a benefit to taking SAMe, but the studies were small and have not been widely accepted by scientists.

Omega-3 fatty acids are found in foods such as fish. People take omega-3 fatty acid supplements to combat depressive symptoms. Some small studies found positive results, but a large study of 1,400 people found the benefit too small to mean much. More studies are needed on SAMe and omega-3 fatty acids to assess their effectiveness on depressive symptoms.

recounting a story of having his tooth pulled. After the dentist visit, he felt low in mood. He had very dark thoughts about death. He wanted to isolate himself from other people and sleep. These are some of the symptoms of depressive disorders. In retrospect, Bullmore wondered if these symptoms were linked to his immune system reaction and inflammation in his mouth.

Bullmore discusses rat research that indicates an association between the immune system and depression. The rats were injected with bacteria, which activated their immune systems. They demonstrated sickness behavior similar to depressive symptoms. The rats withdrew from social contact. Their eating

St. John's Wort

St. John's Wort is a plant. Some people use St. John's Wort as a supplement to treat depression. According to the National Center for Complementary and Integrative Health, the studies on the effectiveness of St. John's Wort for depression are mixed. One concern is that the supplement interacts with certain medications and makes them less effective, including birth control pills, the blood thinner Warfarin, and the HIV medication indinavir. In addition, St. John's Wort increases serotonin levels and can interact with medications that also increase serotonin, posing a possibly life-threatening complication. Whenever patients consider taking supplements, they should be sure to ask a physician about them.

and sleeping habits were disturbed. They weren't physically active.

Interferons also pointed scientists to a connection between the immune system and depression. Interferons were often prescribed for patients with chronic hepatitis. Interferons boost the immune system, and patients taking interferons frequently had depressive symptoms. Another curious connection between depression and the immune system is that patients who have autoimmune diseases, such as type 1 diabetes, also have a higher risk of depression. Autoimmune diseases occur when the immune system turns upon a person's own cells instead of attacking foreign bodies.

Laughter and Depression

Laughter has healing effects on the body and brain. According to the Harvard Mahoney Neuroscience Institute, studies show that laughter has physical benefits. It reduces stress and boosts the immune system. In addition, laughter improves blood flow. In the brain, laughter releases dopamine, serotonin, and endorphins.

Neuroimmune Research

Georgia Hodes, Veronika Kana, and their colleagues have written about current research concerning the connection between the immune system and depression. They say that the correlation was found decades ago when researchers noted "increased levels of circulating inflammatory cytokines in depression."[4] They add that patients with major depressive disorder have higher levels of inflammatory markers and greater numbers of circulating leukocytes, or white blood cells.

Researchers are studying whether the use of anti-inflammatory drugs can reduce depressive symptoms. Some studies have found that the anti-inflammatory medication infliximab, often prescribed for autoimmune diseases, can improve depressive symptoms in depressed patients with high levels of inflammatory markers in their blood. Other studies found an improvement in depressed patients using nonsteroidal anti-inflammatory drugs (NSAIDs). In these studies, the NSAID celecoxib has been found to be particularly effective in reducing depressive symptoms.

Deep Brain Stimulation

Deep brain stimulation (DBS) is a surgical intervention that has FDA approval for treatment of movement disorders, such as Parkinson's disease and essential tremor. Clinical trials are studying whether DBS might be effective with treatment-resistant depression. In DBS, a neurostimulator similar to a pacemaker is implanted near the patient's collarbone. The neurostimulator is attached to electrodes planted in specific areas of the brain. Intermittent electrical impulses are sent from the neurostimulator to the electrodes.

Beginning in 2005, Helen Mayberg, then a professor at Emory University and now a professor at Icahn School of Medicine at Mount Sinai, was involved in clinical trials of DBS for patients with treatment-resistant depression. Mayberg found that

During deep brain stimulation surgery, patients are asked to follow instructions to help doctors assess their brain function.

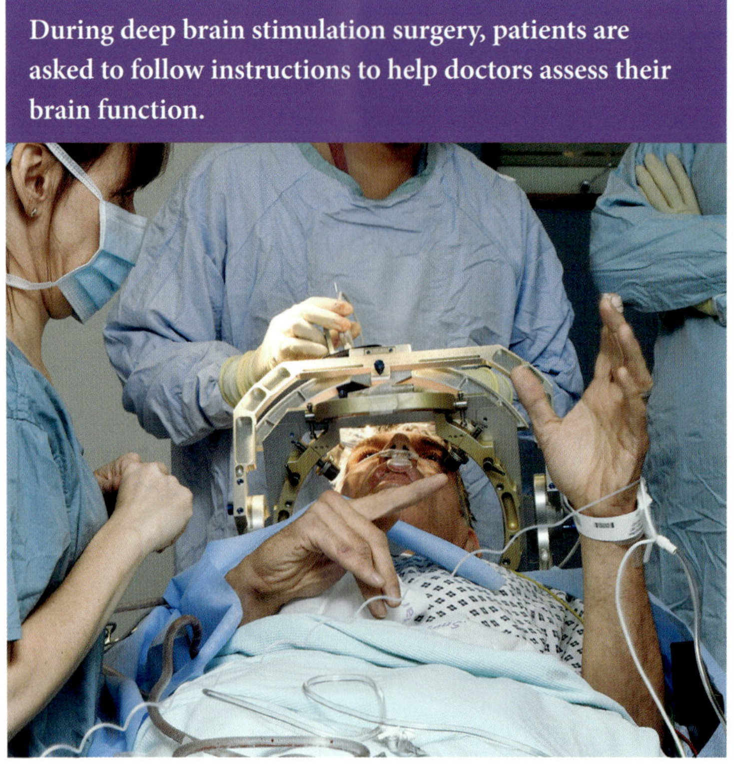

a particular region of the brain, known as Brodmann area 25, was especially active in depressed individuals. In her clinical trials, patients with severe depression had the electrodes implanted in area 25. Mayberg's initial small trials proved promising. Twenty-eight participants were studied for an eight-year period following the trials. The antidepressant effects of the DBS targeting area 25 were "robust and sustained," says Mayberg. The researchers noted, "Response and remission rates were maintained at or above 50 percent and 30 percent, respectively, through years two through eight of the follow-up period."[5] More research focusing on DBS treatment for depression is being done.

Depression is a serious mental illness. No matter the specific type of depressive disorder with which a person is diagnosed, it presents daily difficulties and challenges. But there is every reason to hope for recovery when presented with a diagnosis of depression. Many effective treatments exist for depression, and there are more promising treatments being studied.

"So that's the real message of hope, is that you can get better."[6]

—Andrew Solomon, author of The Noonday Demon: An Atlas of Depression

Essential Facts

Facts about Depression

- Depression is a mood disorder. It is one of the most common mental disorders in the United States.
- There are multiple recognized depressive disorder categories, including major depressive disorder, persistent depressive disorder (dysthymia), premenstrual dysphoric disorder, substance/medication-induced depressive disorder, depressive disorder due to another medical condition, and disruptive mood dysregulation disorder.
- Genetic, environmental, biological, and psychological factors are all linked to depression.

How Depression Affects Daily Life

- Depression can affect an individual's relationships with family and friends. Often people with depression isolate themselves.
- People with depression might have difficulty at their jobs or in school. There might be frequent absences. Their fatigue or lack of concentration might affect their productivity.
- Depression might cause people to sleep much of the day. On the other hand, some people with depression have trouble falling asleep or staying asleep.
- Some people with depression consider suicide. Others attempt to kill themselves. In this way, depression can be a life-threatening disorder.

How Depression Can Be Treated

- The most effective treatment for many patients' depression is a combination of antidepressant medication and psychotherapy.
- Most antidepressant medications target the level of neurotransmitters in the brain. Serotonin, norepinephrine, dopamine, and glutamate are the main neurotransmitters that antidepressants make more available in the brain.
- Cognitive behavioral therapy (CBT) and dialectical behavior therapy (DBT) are effective treatments for depression.
- For treatment-resistant depression, electroconvulsive shock therapy (ECT) provides a quick and reliable treatment for depression. Repetitive transcranial magnetic stimulation (rTMS) and vagus nerve stimulation (VNS) are also sometimes used.
- People diagnosed with depression can help themselves by eating a healthy diet, exercising, getting regular sleep, and socializing. Mindfulness is a helpful technique as well.

Quote

"You may feel skeptical or even pessimistic that anything can help you. . . . Even if you're feeling pessimistic, consider that it may be the depression itself that is making you pessimistic, and so it may take treating the disorder first in order to change your thinking."

—Lee H. Coleman, author of *Depression: A Guide to the Newly Diagnosed.*

Glossary

acute

Strong and often short-lived.

anesthetic

A substance that causes a loss of consciousness or an insensitivity to pain; used to reduce suffering during surgical procedures.

augmented

Added or expanded.

chronic

Continuing for a long time.

cognitive

Related to the act or process of thinking, reasoning, remembering, imagining, or learning.

differentiate

To recognize the dissimilarities or differences.

dysphoric

Feeling very unhappy, uneasy, or dissatisfied.

heritability

A measure of how much genetics account for a particular trait.

impairment

Diminishment or loss of function or ability.

intoxication

The condition of having physical or mental control sharply diminished by the effects of drugs or alcohol.

pessimistic

Characterized by the belief that the worst will happen.

prevalence

How widely present something is.

stigma

A set of negative and often unfair beliefs that a society or group of people has about something.

trauma

An emotionally disturbing or distressing event.

Additional Resources

Selected Bibliography

Bullmore, Edward. *The Inflamed Mind: A Radical New Approach to Depression*. Picador, 2019.

Chokroverty, Linda, MD, FAAP. *100 Questions & Answers about Your Child's Depression or Bipolar Disorder*. Jones and Bartlett, 2010.

Coleman, Lee H., PhD. *Depression: A Guide for the Newly Diagnosed*. New Harbinger, 2012.

Further Readings

Harris, Duchess, JD, PhD, with Rebecca Morris. *The Health-Care Divide*. Abdo, 2019.

Parks, Peggy. *Kids and Mental Illness*. ReferencePoint, 2019.

Steffens, Bradley. *The Suicide Epidemic*. ReferencePoint, 2020.

Online Resources

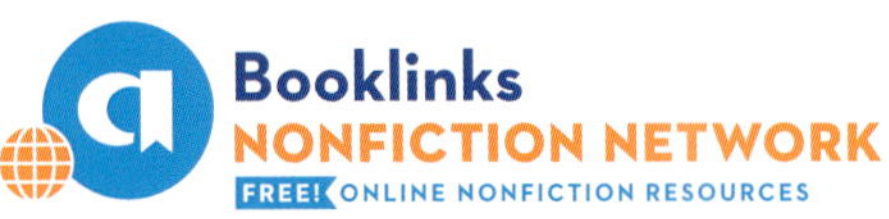

To learn more about handling depression, please visit **abdobooklinks.com** or scan this QR code. These links are routinely monitored and updated to provide the most current information available.

More Information

For more information on this subject, contact or visit the following organizations:

American Psychiatric Association

800 Maine Ave. SW, Ste. 900
Washington, DC 20024
888-357-7924
psychiatry.org
The American Psychiatric Association is a professional organization of psychiatrists. The organization's mission is to provide humane and effective treatment to those with mental illness and to promote mental illness education and research.

National Alliance on Mental Illness

4301 Wilson Blvd., Ste. 300
Arlington, VA 22203
703-524-7600
nami.org
The National Alliance on Mental Illness (NAMI) is the largest grassroots mental health organization in the United States. The organization advocates for and educates those with mental illness and their families.

National Institute of Mental Health

Office of Science Policy, Planning, and Communications
6001 Executive Blvd., Rm. 6200, MSC 9663
Bethesda, MD 20892
866-615-6464
nimh.nih.gov
The National Institute of Mental Health is the lead US federal agency for research on mental disorders.

Source Notes

CHAPTER 1. WHAT IS DEPRESSION?

1. Michelle Quilter. Personal interview. 3 May 2020.

2. Lee H. Coleman. *Depression: A Guide for the Newly Diagnosed*. New Harbinger, 2012. 10.

3. Coleman, *Depression: A Guide for the Newly Diagnosed*, 40.

4. Quilter, Personal interview.

CHAPTER 2. MAJOR AND PERSISTENT DEPRESSIVE DISORDERS

1. Patrick W. Corrigan and Amy C. Watson. "Understanding the Impact of Stigma on People with Mental Illness." *World Psychiatry*, Feb. 2002, ncbi.nlm.nih.gov. Accessed 25 Aug. 2020.

2. Debra J. Brody et al. "Prevalence of Depression among Adults Aged 20 and Over: United States, 2013–2016." *CDC*, Feb. 2018, cdc.gov. Accessed 25 Aug. 2020.

3. American Psychiatric Association. *Depressive Disorders: DSM-5 Selections*. American Psychiatric Publishing, 2015. 11.

4. Keith Kramlinger. *Mayo Clinic on Depression*. Mason Crest, 2001. 174.

5. *Depressive Disorders*, 18.

6. Michelle Quilter. Personal interview. 3 May 2020.

7. Quilter, Personal interview.

CHAPTER 3. OTHER DEPRESSIVE DISORDERS

1. Jennifer Payne. "Can Menopause Cause Depression?" *Johns Hopkins Medicine*, n.d., hopkinsmedicine.org. Accessed 25 Aug. 2020.

2. Sabrina Hofmeister and Seth Bodden. "Premenstrual Syndrome and Premenstrual Dysphoric Disorder." *American Family Physician*, 1 Aug. 2016, aafp.org. Accessed 25 Aug. 2020.

3. Hofmeister and Bodden, "Premenstrual Syndrome and Premenstrual Dysphoric Disorder."

4. Susan J. Noonan. *Managing Your Depression: What You Can Do to Feel Better*. Johns Hopkins University Press, 2013. 24.

5. American Psychiatric Association. *Depressive Disorders: DSM-5 Selections*. American Psychiatric Publishing, 2015. 27.

6. Lee H. Coleman. *Depression: A Guide for the Newly Diagnosed*. New Harbinger, 2012. 13.

7. Vani Rao. "Neuropsychiatry of Stroke." *Johns Hopkins Medicine*, n.d., hopkinsmedicine.org. Accessed 25 Aug. 2020.

8. *Depressive Disorders*, 2.

CHAPTER 4. PINPOINTING A DIAGNOSIS

1. Deborah Serani. *Depression in Later Life: An Essential Guide*. Rowman & Littlefield, 2016. 2.

2. Matthew Griepp. Personal interview. 2 May 2020.

3. "Major Depressive Disorder with Peripartum Onset." *NAMI*, Aug. 2017, nami.org. Accessed 25 Aug. 2020.

4. "Postpartum Depression." *Office on Women's Health*, 14 May 2019, womenshealth.gov. Accessed 25 Aug. 2020.

5. "Almost Half of All Postpartum Psychosis Are Isolated Cases." *ScienceDaily*, 20 Apr. 2020, sciencedaily.com. Accessed 25 Aug. 2020.

6. "Seasonal Affective Disorder." *NIMH*, Mar. 2016, nimh.nih.gov. Accessed 25 Aug. 2020.

7. Ann West [pseud.]. Personal Interview. 30 Apr. 2020.

CHAPTER 5. RISK FACTORS

1. Kenneth S. Kendler et al. "A Swedish National Twin Study of Lifetime Major Depression." *American Journal of Psychiatry*, 2006, ajp.psychiatryonline.org. Accessed 25 Aug. 2020.

2. Eugene S. Paykel. "Basic Concept of Depression." *Dialogues in Clinical Neuroscience*, Sept. 2008, ncbi.nlm.nih.gov. Accessed 25 Aug. 2020.

3. Paykel, "Basic Concept of Depression."

4. Roy C. Ziegelstein. "Depression and Heart Disease." *Johns Hopkins Medicine*, n.d., hopkinsmedicine.org. Accessed 25 Aug. 2020.

5. "Depression." *American Cancer Society*, 1 Feb. 2020, cancer.org. Accessed 25 Aug. 2020.

6. "Depression." *NAMI*, Aug. 2017, nami.org. Accessed 25 Aug. 2020.

Source Notes *Continued*

7. Edward Bullmore. *The Inflamed Mind: A Radical New Approach to Depression*. Picador, 2018. 55.

8. "Suicide in America: Frequently Asked Questions." *NIH*, n.d., nimh.nih.gov. Accessed 25 Aug. 2020.

9. Matthew Griepp. Personal interview. 2 May 2020.

10. Griepp, Personal interview.

CHAPTER 6. CURRENT TREATMENTS

1. American Psychiatric Association. *Depressive Disorders: DSM-5 Selections*. American Psychiatric Publishing, 2015. xi.

2. "Types of Medication." *NAMI*, Aug. 2017, nami.org. Accessed 25 Aug. 2020.

3. Matthew Griepp. Personal interview. 2 May 2020.

4. Griepp, Personal interview.

5. Keith Kramlinger. *Mayo Clinic on Depression*. Mason Crest, 2001. 87.

6. Michelle Quilter. Personal interview. 3 May 2020.

7. "Depression: Out of the Shadows." *PBS*, 2008, pbs.org. Accessed 25 Aug. 2020.

8. Quilter, Personal interview.

9. "Electroconvulsive Therapy (ECT)." *Mayo Clinic*, 12 Oct. 2018, mayoclinic.org. Accessed 25 Aug. 2020.

10. Griepp, Personal interview.

11. "Brain Stimulation Therapies." *NIH*, n.d., nimh.nih.gov. Accessed 25 Aug. 2020.

12. "Brain Stimulation Therapies."

CHAPTER 7. LIVING WITH DEPRESSION

1. May Wolfe [pseud.]. Personal interview. 18 Apr. 2020.

2. Wolfe [pseud.], Personal interview.

3. Deborah Serani. "Depression and Non-Suicidal Self Injury." *Psychology Today*, 28 Feb. 2012, psychologytoday.com. Accessed 25 Aug. 2020.

4. Wolfe [pseud.], Personal interview.

5. Wolfe [pseud.], Personal interview.

6. Wolfe [pseud.], Personal interview.

7. Wolfe [pseud.], Personal interview.

8. Ann West [pseud.]. Personal Interview. 30 Apr. 2020.

9. "The Complex Relationship between Sleep, Depression, and Anxiety." *SleepFoundation.org,* 28 July 2020, sleepfoundation.org. Accessed 25 Aug. 2020.

10. Wolfe [pseud.], Personal interview.

11. West [pseud.], Personal interview.

12. West [pseud.], Personal interview.

13. "Exercise Is an All-Natural Treatment to Fight Depression." *Harvard Health Publishing*, 25 Mar. 2019, health.harvard.edu. Accessed 25 Aug. 2020.

14. "Exercise Is an All-Natural Treatment to Fight Depression."

CHAPTER 8. TREATMENTS ON THE HORIZON

1. Robert C. Meisner. "Ketamine for Major Depression: New Tool, New Questions." *Harvard Health Publishing*, 22 May 2019, health.harvard.edu. Accessed 25 Aug. 2020.

2. R. L. Carhart-Harris et al. "Psilocybin with Psychological Support for Treatment-Resistant Depression: Six-Month Follow-Up." *Psychopharmacology*, 8 Nov. 2017, link.springer.com. Accessed 25 Aug. 2020.

3. Carhart-Harris et al., "Psilocybin with Psychological Support."

4. Amisha Patel. "Review: The Role of Inflammation in Depression." *Psychiatria Danubina,* Sept. 2013, researchgate.net. Accessed 25 Aug. 2020.

5. "Deep Brain Stimulation Effective to Relieve Treatment-Resistant Depression, Long-Term Data Shows." *Emory News Center*, 4 Oct. 2019, news.emory.edu. Accessed 25 Aug. 2020.

6. "Depression: Out of the Shadows." *PBS*, 2008, pbs.org. Accessed 25 Aug. 2020.

Index

About the Author

Marie-Therese Miller, PhD

Marie-Therese Miller, PhD, is a nonfiction author of books for children and teens. Her most recent books include *Dealing with Psychotic Disorders*, *Understanding Friendship*, and *Feeling Good About You*.

Miller holds a PhD in English from St. John's University, where the focus of her dissertation was James Thurber and humor. She and her husband, John, have five children and a grandson.

About the Consultant

Dr. Carla Marie Manly

Dr. Carla Marie Manly, a clinical psychologist and wellness expert, makes her home in Sonoma County, California. In addition to her clinical practice, she is deeply invested in her roles as author, consultant, advocate, and speaker. With a holistic, body-mind-spirit approach, Dr. Manly specializes in the treatment of anxiety, depression, trauma, and relationship issues. Blending traditional psychotherapy with alternative mindfulness practices, Dr. Manly knows the importance of creating healthy balance, awareness, and positivity. Her motto is this: "A well-lived life is a journey of consciously crafting the best version of oneself. Wellness and joy do not occur by chance; they are fostered by manifesting one's true light with courage and strength. Overall well-being occurs by creating a respectful, aware relationship with oneself and others." Dr. Manly's highly acclaimed books, *Joy from Fear, Date Smart,* and *Aging Joyfully*, offer life-changing insights and tips to help readers create positive, purpose-driven lives.